Culture and Customs
of Zambia

Zambia. Cartography by Bookcomp, Inc.

Culture and Customs of Zambia

∾∾

SCOTT D. TAYLOR

Culture and Customs of Africa
Toyin Falola, Series Editor

GREENWOOD PRESS
Westport, Connecticut • London

Library of Congress Cataloging-in-Publication Data

Taylor, Scott D., 1965–
   Culture and customs of Zambia / Scott D. Taylor.
      p. cm. — (Culture and customs of Africa, ISSN 1530–8367)
   Includes bibliographical references and index.
   ISBN 0–313–33246–0 (alk. paper)
   1. Ethnology—Zambia. 2. Zambia—Social life and customs. I. Title.
GN657.R4T39 2006
306'.096894—dc22   2006023773

British Library Cataloguing in Publication Data is available.

Library of Congress Catalog Card Number: 2006023773
ISBN: 0–313–33246–0
ISSN: 1530–8367

First published in 2006

Greenwood Press, 88 Post Road West, Westport, CT 06881
An imprint of Greenwood Publishing Group, Inc.
www.greenwood.com

Printed in the United States of America

The paper used in this book complies with the
Permanent Paper Standard issued by the National
Information Standards Organization (Z39.48–1984).

10 9 8 7 6 5 4 3 2 1

Contents

For my sons,

Chilamo Muntemba and Chali Mulenga

So that they may know their heritage.

Series Foreword

Africa is a vast continent, the second largest, after Asia. It is four times the size of the United States, excluding Alaska. It is the cradle of human civilization. A diverse continent, Africa has more than fifty countries with a population of over 700 million people who speak over 1,000 languages. Ecological and cultural differences vary from one region to another. As an old continent, Africa is one of the richest in culture and customs, and its contributions to world civilization are impressive indeed.

Africans regard culture as essential to their lives and future development. Culture embodies their philosophy, worldview, behavior patterns, arts, and institutions. The books in this series intend to capture the comprehensiveness of African culture and customs, dwelling on such important aspects as religion, worldview, literature, media, art, housing, architecture, cuisine, traditional dress, gender, marriage, family, lifestyles, social customs, music, and dance.

The uses and definitions of "culture" vary, reflecting its prestigious association with civilization and social status, its restriction to attitude and behavior, its globalization, and the debates surrounding issues of tradition, modernity, and postmodernity. The participating authors have chosen a comprehensive meaning of culture while not ignoring the alternative uses of the term.

Each volume in the series focuses on a single country, and the format is uniform. The first chapter presents a historical overview, in addition to information on geography, economy, and politics. Each volume then proceeds to examine the various aspects of culture and customs. The series highlights the mechanisms for the transmission of tradition and culture across generations: the significance of orality, traditions, kinship rites, and family property distribution; the rise of print culture; and the impact of educational institutions. The series also explores the intersections between local, regional, national, and global bases for identity and social relations. While the volumes are organized nationally, they pay attention to ethnicity and language groups and the links between Africa and the wider world.

The books in the series capture the elements of continuity and change in culture and customs. Custom is not represented as static or as a museum artifact, but as a dynamic phenomenon. Furthermore, the authors recognize the current challenges to traditional wisdom, which include gender relations; the negotiation of local identities in relation to the state; the significance of struggles for power at national and local levels and their impact on cultural traditions and community-based forms of authority; and the tensions between agrarian and industrial/manufacturing/oil-based economic modes of production.

Africa is a continent of great changes, instigated mainly by Africans but also through influences from other continents. The rise of youth culture, the penetration of the global media, and the challenges to generational stability are some of the components of modern changes explored in the series. The ways in which traditional (non-Western and nonimitative) African cultural forms continue to survive and thrive, that is, how they have taken advantage of the market system to enhance their influence and reproductions also receive attention.

Through the books in this series, readers can see their own cultures in a different perspective, understand the habits of Africans, and educate themselves about the customs and cultures of other countries and people. The hope is that the readers will come to respect the cultures of others and see them not as inferior or superior to theirs, but merely as different. Africa has always been important to Europe and the United States, essentially as a source of labor, raw materials, and markets. Blacks are in Europe and the Americas as part of the African diaspora, a migration that took place primarily due to the slave trade. Recent African migrants increasingly swell their number and visibility. It is important to understand the history of the diaspora and the newer migrants, as well as the roots of the culture and customs of the places from where they come. It is equally important to understand others in order to be able to interact successfully in a world that keeps shrinking. The accessible nature of the books in this series will contribute to this understanding and enhance the quality of human interaction in a new millennium.

Toyin Falola
Frances Higginbothom, Nalle Centennial Professor in History
The University of Texas at Austin

Preface

Zambia stands out in Africa as one of the continent's most peaceful countries. In its early years as an independent state, Zambia became a regional bulwark against imperialism and colonial domination and South African apartheid. Today, it is looked upon as an important example of Africa's democratization in the last 15 years, experiencing both incredible success as well as some notable setbacks. The country is also one of the most urbanized in sub-Saharan Africa, a phenomenon that began with the colonial era gravitation toward the central mining regions of Zambia's Copperbelt. As a result of this urban influx, Zambia's diverse ethnolinguistic groups interact regularly. Moreover, many contemporary Zambian households, especially those in cities, are also exposed to the media, technology, and influences of Western urbanized cultures, from Internet cafes to hip-hop music. In other words, notions of tradition and modernity conflict and combine in interesting ways in contemporary Zambia. Not surprisingly, for all these reasons, scholars from a variety of disciplines have been fascinated by Zambia's political, economic, and social-development experiences, and the challenges thereto, because the country offers unique insights as well as important lessons for the rest of Africa. This book explores Zambia's culture, with an eye toward its historical experiences and its particular endowments. It focuses on how traditional and modern interact, and sometimes collide, in the country.

Among Zambia's 73 ethnolinguistic communities, the major groups are examined to give the reader an idea about how many Zambians live and have tried to navigate the pressures of a changing country. As noted, the urban environment has produced an amalgam of traditional and modern where different groups mix socially, linguistically, and in any variety of professional and personal contexts. Thus, the customs in Zambia's urban zones have become increasingly homogenized to an important degree. Where traditional customs are maintained—in cities and certainly in rural areas—I endeavor to point out those that are unique to a particular group as well as those that are representative of customs that are shared by diverse groups of people.

As the subsequent chapters will show, a variety of geographical, historical, and political influences impact culture and customs in Zambia. Interestingly, culture and customs both are undergoing profound changes and revealing important continuities at the same time. The continued flight to cities, typically in search of employment, for example, has increased citizens' exposure to more Western ideas and influences. Zambia's recent transition to a more democratic form of government has increased opportunities for social interaction and public expression. Zambia remains essentially "Zambian," however, in the sense that the character of its citizens is unique within the region and within Africa as a whole.

In Zambia today, as in much of Africa, tradition and modernity not only exist side by side, but also what is modern becomes thoroughly endogenized, and the traditional is altered and adapted as well. Therefore, although many of the chapters and headings that follow are subdivided into traditional and modern categories, readers should be aware that this is, in many ways, a false dichotomy. In fact, it is a largely U.S., or at least Western, way of conceptualizing contemporary life. What one sees, then, is a uniquely Zambian combination of elements—in politics, religion, social relations, and so forth. Culture is inherently fluid, and so it is in Zambia; people adopt new customs and characteristics as a result of exposure to different groups and different customs. Western and other non-Zambian norms are introduced by travel, music, television, and the arts. Cultural ceremonies die or fade from memory, whereas long-dormant ones are revived and help rekindle a sense of identity, such as the Umutomboko ceremony of the Lunda people.

By the same token, intra-Zambian norms are shared as a result of the inculcation of a thoroughly national identity. Although this identity was initially imposed artificially through colonialism, a collective sense of so-called Zambianness was later forged out of necessity by President Kaunda and the postcolonial government. Indeed, consider that in precolonial times, the Lozi people had scant knowledge of their Bemba counterparts; today they interact regularly in social, economic, and political forums.

Finally, examples abound of the merging of cultures and customs, both intra-Zambian and between Zambian and Western traditions and practices. Christianity is pervasive, though it incorporates indigenous traditions in some locales; English is the first language of many middle class urban children; traditional, historically secretive wedding rites are now commonly captured on that most essential of modern devices, video; urban dialects of Nyanja and Bemba language are increasingly sprinkled with English words so as to form altogether new speech patterns; the cultural ceremonies of one ethnic group are adopted, modified, and incorporated into those of another (e.g., such that the marriage ritual *amatebeto* becomes a Zambian cultural tradition as much as a Bemba one). In short, these new customs, habits—indeed, traditions— thus become thoroughly embedded, and the culture adapts to accommodate them. These are the issues that make the study of the culture and customs of Zambia so compelling and dynamic.

Acknowledgments

This project benefited from the input and support of a number of people. First and foremost, I would like to thank Professor Toyin Falola for inviting me to contribute this volume to the Culture and Customs of Africa series, and for the encouragement and helpful comments he provided along the way. Wendi Schnaufer, a senior acquisitions editor at Greenwood Publishing, ably and patiently guided the process from the beginning and I greatly appreciated her forbearance when I *occasionally* missed a deadline; I am particularly grateful for her willingness to offer positive feedback, despite the havoc I wrought on her schedule. Also at Greenwood, Kaitlin Ciarmello oversaw the final chapters of the manuscript and saw the project to fruition. It was a pleasure to work with them on this book.

Certainly, the road to completion of the book would have been considerably more difficult without the contributions of Kennji Kizuka and Nick Morin, two Georgetown students who helped me track down several particularly elusive sources and provided exceptional research assistance overall. Although most of the photographs in the book are mine, Megan Simon Thomas kindly agreed to provide two from her collection. I would also like to thank my friend Dr. Lise Rakner, one of the foremost experts on contemporary Zambian politics, for sharing with me her invaluable insights. Our always informative and stimulating discussions over nearly 10 years have helped shape my own interpretations of Zambian politics and society. Dr. Nancy Chongo Kula was always willing to lend assistance, particularly in interpreting certain Bemba stories and expressions. I am particularly grateful to Hilary Mulenga Fyfe whose knowledge of Zambian history and cultural traditions is rivaled only by her commitment to their preservation. She kindly provided materials from Zambia, and even more valuably, offered her rich insight gleaned from years of experience as an activist, consultant, and commissioner in Zambia.

In the past 15 years, I have been privileged to become acquainted with many Zambian people and their practices, from both a scholarly perspective as well as a personal one. I have traveled throughout the country and, as a result, have witnessed and experienced many of the customs and traditions, old and new, described in this book. My deepest gratitude, therefore, goes to the people of Zambia, who over the years have so generously welcomed me into their fold.

Finally, I would like to thank my family for their love and support. My wife, Priscilla Muntemba, went beyond her spousal duties by commenting on several of the chapters. My two young sons, Chilamo and Chali, endured my absence more times than was fair. I hope that sometime in the not-too distant future, when they are old enough to read the dedication to this book, they will be willing to overlook the transgression.

Chronology

1100	Bantu migration displaces indigenous San peoples.
1200	Tonga and Ila peoples migrate from the east.
1500s–1750	Fragments of the Luba and Lunda empires in Congo migrate to Zambia, forming new kingdoms; the Bemba, Bisa, Lovale, Kaonde, Lamba, Lunda, and Lozi emerge.
1851	First visit to area by the Scottish missionary and explorer David Livingstone.
1889–90	British South Africa Company (BSA) establishes control over Northern Rhodesia (Zambia).
1924	BSA cedes control over Northern Rhodesia to British Colonial Office.
1953–63	Federation is established between colonial territories of Northern and Southern Rhodesia and Nyassaland.
1962	Civil disobedience accelerates moves toward independence.
1964, October 24	Independence.
1972, December	One Party Declaration is enacted.

1980s	Copper prices plunge; debt increases.
1985	Zambia adopts comprehensive economic adjustment program with International Monetary Fund and World Bank.
1986–87	Food riots.
1987, May	The Structural Adjustment Program SAP is abandoned unilaterally by Zambia.
1989, June	New SAP is initiated; abolishes price controls, except on staples
1990, June	Food riots.
1990, June	Reports of an attempted coup against Kaunda precipitate widespread public celebration.
1990, July	Movement for Multiparty Democracy (MMD) coalition is established.
1990, December	Parliament approves multiparty option.
1991, June	Reintroduction of price controls by the United National Independence Party (UNIP) weakens SAP.
1991, September	Adjustment program is suspended again.
1991, October 31	MMD wins, and Frederick Chiluba is elected president.
1992, January	Structural Adjustment Program is reinstated.
1992–93	Worst drought in a century hits southern Africa.
1993, March	A state of emergency is declared in response to an alleged plot to overthrow the government (state of emergency lasts three months).
1994–95	Severe drought again hits the region.
1996, May–June	UNIP opposition leaders are arrested for alleged involvement in a plot called Black Mamba. Charges are eventually dropped.
1996, June	Former President Kenneth Kaunda is barred from standing for reelection.

1996, November 18	Controversial second elections are held. UNIP and several other opposition parties boycott. Chiluba wins 73 percent of the vote; MMD wins 131 seats; Independents win 10 seats; other parties win 9 seats.
1997, October	Coup attempt by a disgruntled army captain. Despite no evidence of their involvement, Kenneth Kaunda and other opposition leaders are arrested and charged with conspiracy and treason.
1998, February–December	Treason trial. Kaunda is released without charge in March.
1998	Government agrees to sell most of the mining industry to Anglo American Corporation.
1998, November	Former Finance Minister Ronald Penza is assassinated.
1998, December	Former business executive Anderson Mazoka launches the United Party for National Development.
2001, February	Acting under a body called the Oasis Forum, civic groups mobilize against a prospective third-term bid by President Chiluba.
2001, April	MMD Party Congress alters party constitution to allow a third term for the president.
2001, May	Chiluba abandons his bid after pressure from the Oasis Forum, wider civil society, and former cabinet members.
2001, August	Chiluba names lawyer and one-time vice president Levy Mwanawasa as the MMD presidential candidate and his putative successor.
2001, December	Mwanawasa defeats Mazoka by 28.7 percent to 26.7 percent in the presidential election.
2002, January	Opposition parties file a legal challenge with the High Court contesting the Mwanawasa/MMD victory.
2002, July	Parliament removes former President Chiluba's immunity from prosecution.

2003, February	Chiluba arrested and charged on 59 counts, including abuse of office.
2003, August	Chiluba charged with the theft of more than $30 million during his term in office.
2003	Severe drought puts up to three million people at risk. Facing enormous criticism from donors and others, President Mwanawasa refuses the offer of genetically modified (GMO) food aid on the grounds that it may be harmful.
2003, December	Chiluba's trial on corruption charges begins.
2005, February	The Supreme Court rules against the 2002 challenge to Mwanawasa's election.
2005	Zambia is again hit by severe drought.

1

Introduction—Land, People, and History

Zambia lies at the so-called heart of Africa; although attempts to liken the country's rough dimensions to a heart shape are somewhat forced, its location in the central southern part of the continent clearly lends support to the claim. Indeed, Zambia has much to commend it. With its tropical climate moderated in much of its territory by high altitude, Zambia is also a land of great geographic diversity. This diversity extends to its people as well. It is a country of rich social and cultural traditions and a long history. Zambia's population of just less than 11 million in 2004 makes it one of the less populous countries of Africa, yet with a land area of 754,000 square kilometers (291,000 square miles), roughly the size of Texas, it has a very low population density. Throughout human history, competition for scarce resources—water, land, and so forth—has been one of the major causes of conflict. Zambia's land abundance, however, is an important factor in explaining its reputation as a peaceful country; unlike many countries in Africa, it has no modern history of war or major sociopolitical conflict, and this is an indelible part of Zambians' lifestyle and existence today.

Zambia gained its independence from the United Kingdom in October 1964, after nearly a century of colonial domination. Independence brought new opportunities as well as new challenges to the country. For example, whereas colonial rule was an oppressive system of governance that could enforce compliance and cooperation, the new government had to find a way to unite Zambia's 73 different ethnolinguistic groups into one nation. It was no easy task, and it was one that brought authoritarian rule and often ethnic violence elsewhere on the continent. Zambia pursued something of a middle path. The country's first postcolonial leader, President Kenneth D. Kaunda, was able to hew to this path through a series of economic and political maneuvers, though Zambia was scarcely democratic in the Western sense and Kaunda's economic policies ultimately proved damaging. The period from independence to the 1990s, then, was characterized by increased concentration of power in the executive and economic policies that were generally retrograde, a course taken by most of the 47 countries in sub-Saharan Africa (SSA). In 1991, Zambia became only the second country in SSA to undergo a multiparty transition to democracy. Importantly, it was Zambia's people, especially urban residents, who mobilized most passionately for change.

The 1990s were characterized by the ebb and flow of democracy and occasional displays by the new government of authoritarian tendencies. Although events unfolded in a context of deepening poverty and growing external dependence on international donors, in general it was a period of increased social freedoms and greater political opportunities for Zambia's people. Zambia, however, is far poorer today than it was a quarter-century ago. The present day, therefore, finds Zambia at something of a crossroads: This early democratizer has shown many promising signs, including elections, rule of law, and institution-building. At the same time, poverty levels, the HIV-AIDS epidemic, and reduction of crucial social services—health, education, child welfare, and so forth—have all been exacerbated by recent trends. It remains to be seen which direction Zambia will take: toward deeper democracy and economic and social development or toward a more ambiguous future. Fortunately, it is unlikely that Zambia—given its natural resources such as ample land and minerals, history of interethnic cooperation, and emerging political pluralism—will ever descend the destructive and violent path taken by some other countries in Africa and elsewhere in the developing world. These features augur positively for Zambia's future.

The land in which people live is inextricably tied to their identity and customs; therefore, we begin this study of Zambia with an examination of the country's land and geographic endowments.

LAND

Landlocked Zambia is surrounded on all sides by an astounding eight countries: Angola, Namibia, Botswana, Zimbabwe, Mozambique, Malawi, Tanzania, and the Democratic Republic of the Congo. This long, substantially unguarded border has created numerous problems for Zambia: refugee flows, external violence in the form of warfare and crime that encroach on Zambia's own stability, as well as illegal smuggling and trade, to name a few.

The country's encirclement also means that Zambia is dependent on its neighbors to a huge degree; most international trade must transverse another state, typically one with access to the sea, thereby increasing the cost of goods imported to Zambia. Moreover, when the entire region was in turmoil and conflict in the 1970s and 1980s (and to a lesser degree until the 1990s), Zambia was often forced to secrete goods into the country to avoid seizure or destruction.

Its peculiar borders, like those of virtually all SSA states, were artificial creations of the leading European powers, which met in the German capital of Berlin in 1884–85 to literally carve up the map of Africa in what is referred to as the Scramble for Africa. As the phrase implies, the scramble was guided less by geographic logic than by the rush to divide Africa's assets as rapidly as possible. Indeed, in most cases, proper surveys of the newly claimed territories were not conducted until well after this three-month-long meeting, which is commonly referred to by historians as the Berlin Conference. (The nature of the Scramble also had dire implications for African peoples, as discussed later.) Zambia's borders, then, make little sense from a geographic (or ethnographic) standpoint. To the south, its border with Zimbabwe is clearly defined: the majestic Zambezi River and the spectacular 108-meter (350-foot) Victoria Falls form a natural boundary. To the northeast, the border with Tanzania is more or less defined by Lake Tanganyika. Conversely, Zambia's other borders, with Angola, the Democratic Republic of the Congo (DRC), Namibia, Malawi, and Mozambique are, by and large, neither marked by natural boundaries nor any other perceptible demarcation or obstacle. In fact, some, such as the DRC and Namibia, appear downright bizarre, a result of rival German, Belgian, and Portuguese jockeying for resources and control during the Berlin Conference.

Despite their relative unimportance to the structure of Zambian political borders, the country boasts an incredible number of significant natural landmarks and geographic features. In addition to the Zambezi River, the country contains some six major rivers and river basins. The Zambezi, which is navigable only in some portions, runs a total of 3,540 kilometer (2,200 miles), from its headwaters in the DRC, along the border with Zimbabwe, and toward Mozambique, where it finally empties into the Indian Ocean. The two other major rivers are the Kafue, which bisects the provinces in the country's center and runs approximately 970 kilometers (600 miles), and the Luangwa River, which flows from Zambia's northeast. Both the Kafue and Luangwa are tributaries of the larger Zambezi in the south.

One of the most impressive landmarks of the Zambian environment is not natural at all: The 5,000-square-kilometer (1,900-square-mile) Lake Kariba was formed in 1958 as a result of a dam on the lower Zambezi River. Straddling the border between Zambia and present-day Zimbabwe, the dam involuntarily displaced at least 30,000 thousand indigenous people, almost entirely of the Tonga ethnic group. More positively, damming the Zambezi not only created a massive refuge for wildlife (and tourism), but its turbine generators also produce much of the region's electricity supply, including to the Zambian Copperbelt, the hub of the economy. Together with Zambia's extensive rivers and other large lakes (Mweru, Bangwelu, and Tanganyika, all in Northern Province), Lake Kariba is also a major site of Zambia's fishing industry.

Zambia lies almost entirely between the 10th and 20th parallels latitude in south-central Africa. The country is situated in the southern tropics, but its altitude—the country is situated mostly on high plateau above 900 meters (3,000 feet)—mitigates against tropical temperatures in most areas. There are some hills and mountains, but none with significant elevation. Zambia's climate ranges from the low humidity zones of Lusaka and the high central plateau to the sultry tropical environment of the Zambezi River valley in the south or in other river basins. The higher altitude regions, of course, are far less prone to tropical diseases, such as malaria and sleeping sickness, a factor that helps explain patterns of European settlement in the country's center. During the colonial period, white settlers, initially from South Africa and later from Southern Rhodesia (Zimbabwe) and Europe, tended to cluster around the more moderate climates in the central part of the country, establishing farms there on lands seized mainly from the Tonga. In the north-central part of the country (Central and Copperbelt Provinces), extensive deposits of copper, cobalt, and other minerals were exploited beginning in the early twentieth century, and substantial mining operations developed there. As a result, the modern infrastructure (road, rail, and telecommunications) of Zambia was centered on this agromining nexus, which also attracted the greatest African immigration and urban settlement.

In contrast, Zambia's far northeastern and western regions can be virtually inaccessible, at least by road, at certain times of the year due to flooding. Rainfall in these areas is in the range of 100–150 centimeters (40–60 inches) per year, and the roads, often poorly built and, in recent years, badly maintained due to prohibitive costs, regularly wash out during Zambia's rainy season, which typically begins in December and ends in March.

The rains can be unpredictable, however, and climatic change as well as environmental degradation (globally, such as from the effects of El Niño and La Niña, and locally due to deforestation) have both contributed to a high incidence of drought in the country. In the Southern Province, for example, rainfall ranges from 64 centimeters to 100 centimeters (25 inches to 40 inches) but can vary by as much as 30 percent per year. In a country where 600,000 peasant farmers and their extended families are dependent on subsistence

farming, these frequent droughts can have devastating impact by increasing food aid dependence and forcing people to migrate to urban areas.

Most of Zambia's soil is highly acidic, sandy, and nutrient poor, although much of that in the Central and Southern Provinces is of higher quality (another explanation for their attractiveness to European settlers). Zambia's indigenous vegetation is mostly deciduous *miombe* woodland, which consists of tall grasses, trees, and shrubs and covers two-thirds of the country. The drier regions in the Western Province are more desertlike, and the tropical Zambezi valley supports a wider variety of flora. Much of Zambia's woodland area is also endangered, however, due to degradation and human encroachment; rampant deforestation in the country claims an additional 0.5 percent of these wooded areas each year. This is a result of felling trees for firewood to make charcoal—the only source of energy for warmth, cooking, and bathing in rural areas and even in some urban households—as well as overuse of timber for construction purposes. In addition, among peasant farmers, the traditional practice called *chitemene* (cutting and burning trees and brush to clear for planting and to provide an easy source of nutrients from the ash) has been overused because of both land and population pressures and unavailability of chemical fertilizers. Over time the *chitemene* method actually depletes the soils of nutrients, leaves great swaths of land bare, and fosters erosion and degradation of many rural lands.

Northern Province landscape. Much of Zambia's landscape is mixed woodland and not well suited to agriculture. Courtesy of the author.

When Europeans began to settle in Zambia in the 1890s, they displaced Africans from the highest quality soils. They also brought with them European crops and livestock to grow for commercial purposes. The principal food crop is maize (corn), but commercial growers also produce rice, wheat, and other crops. Tobacco and cotton are also produced for export as well as some local consumption. Only about 20 percent of the land in Zambia is suitable for agriculture, and these areas are mainly concentrated in the south, central, and eastern parts of the country. Crops like wheat and rice, which require irrigation to grow, can be produced only near or adjacent to urban centers with a reliable municipal water supply; not surprisingly only about 1 percent of Zambia's farmland is under irrigation, all of which is in large commercial farms, so imported crops are required to supplement limited local production. Rainfall in Zambia is simply too erratic otherwise. Producing crops outside the main zones is somewhat limited for commercial purposes as much by soil quality as by accessibility.

PEOPLE[1]

Zambia's colonization by the British South Africa Company (under charter from the British Crown) beginning in 1891 and its subsequent settlement by as many as 70,000 whites, mostly of British origin, ensured that English became the official language of the colony. More than simply an administrative language, as European tongues were in some other colonial possessions in Africa, English became widely used, especially in Zambia's urban and industrial zones. In the postcolonial era, English serves as a helpful lingua franca in a country of some 73 ethnolingusitic groups, none of which can claim a majority.

These groups, in turn, fall into a dozen language groups, and though they share some common Bantu-origin words and structures, they are not mutually intelligible. As a result, English is widely spoken throughout the country, and in most schools students are introduced to the language around the first grade. In fact, English has become so hegemonic in Zambia that many urban parents today prefer to speak to their children in English rather than in their indigenous language. Consequently, a number of Zambia's ethnic groups face existential pressure: Those with small populations and dwindling numbers of speakers and vanishing traditions risk extinction in the twenty-first century. The larger groups, however, seem likely to hold on to both their language and their heritage and traditions, if only by sheer force of numbers.

The largest of the ethnic groups is the Bemba, whose communities were based historically in Zambia's Northern and Luapula Provinces. The Bemba, like most of the groups in Zambia, are a matrilineal society, in which inheritance and status were passed from a man to his sister's son. The paramount chief of the Bemba is the Chitimukulu. In precolonial times, the Bemba were known for their rather substantial kingdom and occasional warfare with their

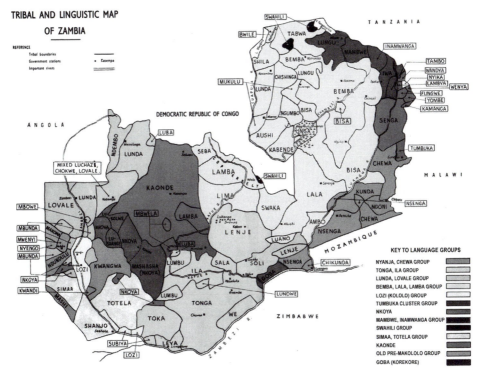

Tribal and linguistic map of Zambia. Anonymous, no date. Lusaka: Surveyor General.

neighbors. Today, they form one of the most politically influential communities in contemporary Zambia, in part because of their population and in part because of their role in the British colonial system. During the colonial period, the Bemba's traditional political structures were undermined by the British, because their proximity to the Copperbelt meant that they were needed to supply much of the labor to the colony's copper-mining operations. Although clearly disadvantaged relative to whites, this exposure ironically placed the Bemba in a more modern, urbanized, and economic position at independence than their counterparts in other groups. A linguistic amalgam substantially based on the Bemba language also became the lingua franca among copper miners, who came from all over the country. In the same vein, although English is the national language of Zambia, given its colonial heritage, Bemba is one of two widely spoken indigenous languages; in fact, it is the primary language of 25 percent of the population, even though ethnic Bemba comprise only about 20 percent of Zambia's population.

The second leading grouping is comprised of the Nyanja-speakers. Nyanja is the first language of about 12 percent of the populace. Importantly, Nyanja speakers are not an ethnic group; the language emerged as a lingua franca, particularly in Lusaka, among a number of groups from Eastern Province. These actually include multiple peoples, such as the Kunda, Ngoni, and Nsenga. In rural areas of Eastern Province, one would encounter much deeper, less contaminated language variants spoken by each of these groups.

The Tonga people, dominant in Zambia's Southern Province also account for 12 percent of first-language speakers. During the colonial era, the Tonga arguably bore the most severe brunt of British settler occupation. Traditionally a vibrant farming culture, much of the Tonga farmland in what is today the Southern and Central Provinces was appropriated for white settlement and farming activity. They were transformed into what has been labeled a *rural proletariat,* serving white landlords on lands formerly owned by the Tonga themselves.[2] Second, the construction of the Kariba Dam on the Zambezi River in the 1950s submerged vast quantities of lands peopled by the Tonga and neighboring groups. Those on both the Zimbabwe and Zambian sides of the border were forcibly relocated to make room for the rising waters. Perhaps not surprisingly, given their abuse at the hands of the colonial state, the Tonga became a force in Zambian politics as early as the founding of the African nationalist movements in the 1950s, and they remain so today.

Finally, among the larger ethno-linguistic groups, the Lozi of Western Province account for some 5.6 percent of all first-language speakers. The Lozi are the heirs to an expansive political kingdom that reached to several contemporary states in the region. Unlike groups like the Bemba and Tonga, the Lozi traditional structures were left largely unfettered by colonialism, and the British administered that territory of the country through a system known as indirect rule. The king of the Lozi people is the Litunga, who presides over an array of chiefs who are affiliated to the royal house. Although many of the historical powers of leaders like the Litunga have been curtailed under the Westernized political structures that prevail today, the Lozi kin and traditional chiefs retain considerable authority and influence within their communities. Moreover, as with other groups, they claim a privileged and respected—often revered—position within the larger community.

It is important to point out that European colonialism, driven by economic greed, territorial conquest, and, to a lesser extent, Christian missionary zeal, had little regard for traditional territories occupied by Africa's ethnic groups. Therefore, Nyanja speakers are found today in Zambia as well as Malawi. Tonga speakers are in Zambia and Zimbabwe. Other groups are similarly divided by Zambia's many other contemporary international borders. Even ethnic Lozi, whose kingdom was left substantially intact by the British, have kinspeople in parts of Namibia and Botswana.

RACIAL PLURALISM

Southern Africa was the major area of white European settlement on the African continent. At their peak, there were substantial white communities in South West Africa (Namibia), South Africa, Northern Rhodesia (Zambia), Southern Rhodesia (Zimbabwe), as well as the Portuguese colonies of Angola and Mozambique. The largest number resided in South Africa, of course, but the others claimed more than one million, in total, under colonial rule. Zambia's white population, which peaked at 73,000 in 1960, was actually among the smallest. By 1995, that population had dwindled to just 30,000 or fewer. Importantly, each of Zambia's regional counterparts experienced an African nationalist rebellion that resulted in varying levels of bloodshed (and sometimes mixed success). Fortunately for Zambia, its colonial period ended quite peacefully, with the transfer of power from the colonial government to the new indigenous government. Although large numbers of whites left at or around independence, those who remained were generally committed to the country and its new black majority.

Today, Zambia's small white population is engaged in industry, the service sector, and commercial farming activities. Unlike the situation in other countries of the region, which experienced protracted liberation struggles that left lingering animosities between blacks and whites, race relations in Zambia have remained quite amicable. Even under colonialism, Zambia maintained better race relations than all of its neighbors, and today whites —and members of Zambia's Asian population—are found serving side by side with blacks on corporate boards, in civic organizations, and even in government. Moreover, it is not uncommon to find speakers with native fluency of Bemba, Tonga, or Nyanja, for example, among many white Zambian families, particularly in the farming sector.

In 2003, some 200 white commercial farmers from neighboring Zimbabwe, displaced by politically motivated racial violence in that country, resettled in Zambia. This followed earlier migrations of smaller numbers of white South African agriculturalists. Whether some of these refugees harbor racist proclivities is impossible to determine—not surprisingly, none would claim that they do—however, their presence has contributed to rising resentments among many Zambians who feel that the white farmers will import Zimbabwe's racial conflicts into Zambia. The fact that the Zambian government has supported this immigration politically and materially (with the goal of increasing the expertise and, thus, productivity of Zambia's previously moribund commercial farming sector) has not helped to allay popular concerns.

This street in Lusaka's Luburma/Madras area is a hub of commercial activity. Most of the shops are owned by Zambians of Asian descent. Courtesy of the author.

HISTORY

Early History

Between 2,500 and 1,000 years ago, Bantu-speaking populations migrated from the western African savannahs through to southern Africa. They eventually merged with, marginalized, and/or pushed out the indigenous Khoisan speakers, generally hunter-gatherer cultures, who themselves settled in the region perhaps 12,000 years ago. Many of the contemporary ethnic groups in Zambia arrived in the territory as recently as 200 to 500 years ago. The Tonga and the Ila are believed to be among the longest resident peoples, arriving from the east in what is now Zambia's Southern Province around A.D. 1200. Most of the other groups followed a southern route; the Lunda, Lovale, Kaonde, Lamba, Lozi (with links to the Lunda), as well as the Bemba and Bisa (descended from the Luba), for example, were offshoots of the great Lunda-Luba Empire in Congo, migrating to Zambia between 1600 and 1750 and establishing their own kingdoms there. It is not known precisely why these migrations took place, but population pressures in the Lualaba River basin in the southern Congo beginning around that time probably played a significant role, along with contact and conflict with Portuguese explorers. The last of the major groups to migrate to what is now Zambia in the precolonial period was the Ngoni, who were an offshoot of the Zulu, fleeing Shaka

Zulu and the white Afrikaner farmers (Boers) in South Africa in the 1820s.

Contact with Western European cultures began with the Portuguese, who became active in the East African trade routes, around 1500. Prior to contact with modern European civilizations, eastern and southern African societies engaged in trade with ancient civilizations in China, Rome, and Arabia at least from the first millennium A.D. The Portuguese slave traders arrived in the region, primarily from the west; Portuguese commercial traders established contacts with Africans from the Indian Ocean.

Historians note frequent clashes between the African peoples who settled in Zambia: between the Bantu speakers and the indigenous Khoisan speakers; between Bemba and Mambwe and Bemba and Bisa people; and between the Ngoni and the Bemba after 1835, when the movement of peoples led to territorial incursions and conflict. Slaves were taken by different groups, and some of these were traded with the Portuguese and Arabs for weapons. The Lozi in the west lived unfettered, however, for much of the time after their settlement in western Zambia's Zambezi floodplain around 1700. Though they dominated many other groups in that area, their conflict with outsiders was limited until 1800, by which time they had developed a highly organized society and kingdom.

The Beginning of the Colonial Period

Beyond accounts of Portuguese incursions, Zambia received scant European attention until the 1850s, when the travels of the Scottish missionary and explorer Dr. David Livingstone, who visited the area as early as 1851, became widely reported in London. Yet not until nearly five years after the Berlin Conference did significant numbers of whites, some as explorers, others as Christian missionaries, begin to arrive in the region. Commercial, political, and religious interests often combined in the larger imperial project of establishing British domination—in southern Africa often indirectly, through the ambitions of the British South Africa Company (BSAC).

Between 1890 and 1891, the BSAC established control over the territory that eventually became known as Zambia. The BSAC used trickery and deception to enter into treaties initially with Lewanika, the Lozi Litunga, in 1890, which gave them an exclusive mining concession in the country in exchange for so-called protection. The company eventually extended its control over the entire territory, again using the dubious concession signed with Lewanika as a pretext for grabbing the entire country of Zambia, including parts in the north and east well beyond Lozi control and influence.

Shortly before duping Lewanika, representatives of the same company had extracted similar concessions from Lewanika's rival King Lobengula of the Ndebele, whose kingdom lay on the southern side of the Zambezi River in what is now Zimbabwe. By 1895, both territories were commonly referred to as Rhodesia, after BSAC magnate Cecil Rhodes; by 1897, the two regions formally became known as Southern Rhodesia and Northern Rhodesia, respectively.

In the first decade of company rule, as BSAC control was extended throughout the territory, limited numbers of whites began to arrive in Northern Rhodesia as settlers, though most worked for the BSAC's growing mining operations. By the turn of the century, greater numbers of whites migrated to Zambia, establishing large farms and other commercial operations. The period of so-called company rule ended in 1923 when the administration of Northern Rhodesia was formally ceded to the Colonial Office in London to administer as a Crown Colony. In fact, the territory had been badly neglected by the BSAC, and there was little infrastructure outside the line of rail in the central part of the country, along which most of the fewer than 5,000 whites had settled by the 1920s. In spite of their small numbers, however, a legislative council was formed that offered Northern Rhodesia's white population the opportunity for representative government. This body then asserted a surprising degree of autonomy from Britain.

The Central African Federation

Almost from their inception, the two Rhodesias shared a number of important linkages, including their common origins as company territories, English-speaking settler populations, and economic ties. Moreover, although both were beholden ultimately to the colonial office in London, each had a substantial degree of autonomy after World War I. Not surprisingly, some combination of the territories, whether through complete administrative and territorial amalgamation or into some type of looser federation, gained serious consideration as early as the 1930s. Yet the Northern Rhodesian and Southern Rhodesian representatives and officials from the Colonial Office were unable to resolve critical debates concerning ultimate sovereignty and, especially, policies governing native populations, which were far harsher in Southern Rhodesia.

By the 1950s, however, these disputes were substantially resolved, and in 1953, Northern Rhodesia and Southern Rhodesia were formally linked, together with Nyasaland (now Malawi), in the Central Africa Federation. In retrospect, it is difficult to ascertain what benefits Zambia and Malawi stood to gain by joining with Southern Rhodesia. The latter had superior infrastructure, established industrial facilities, and well-developed commercial agricultural and mining sectors. Although Northern officials apparently believed that federation would allow them to enjoy immediate benefits and de facto economic diversification by joining with the more industrialized southerners, in reality Southern Rhodesia's superior resource base stayed in Southern Rhodesia. Indeed, Zambian resources—namely copper export revenues—flowed chiefly southward to further Southern Rhodesia's development in the period. The larger white population of Southern Rhodesia thus turned out to be a double-edged sword: Northerners assumed that a greater aggregate settler population would result in greater autonomy from London for the Rhodesias. In reality, however, it meant that Northern Rhodesian, and Malawian, human and natural resources simply enhanced the socioeconomic position of Southern Rhodesian whites.

Each state retained its own national legislatures, and a federal parliament and prime minister were also established, headquartered in Salisbury (now Harare, Zimbabwe). The powers of the federal government were largely limited to defense, trade, communications, industry, and finance. The powers retained by the national governments included local government, African education, health, agriculture, and land policy. Interestingly, Britain was largely relegated to the background in this context. The lack of substantial British intervention meant that the individual governments enjoyed a considerable degree of autonomy over the issues in their purview. This proved particularly problematic in the determination of so-called native policy, which was always among the most highly contested subjects. Although it can hardly be said that colonial rule in Zambia was not repressive—the denial of civil rights and freedoms, alienation from land, and so forth are hallmarks of colonialism, after all—the level of deprivation was far greater among blacks in Southern Rhodesia than in the north. The sheer number of whites residing there—more than 200,000 by 1960—brought them inevitably into conflict with blacks with whom they were competing for resources.

By the early 1960s, the Federation was on its last legs. Done in by the members' irreconcilable approaches to racial policy, it was dissolved in 1963. Britain had acquiesced to majority African rule in both Northern Rhodesia and Malawi. In its short lifetime, the Federation was responsible for substantial economic growth in Zimbabwe, whereas Zambia lost funds that might otherwise have been invested in its own development.

Nationalism and Independence

Influenced by African nationalist movements in Kenya, Ghana, South Africa, and throughout the continent, fledgling nationalist organizations emerged as a powerful movement in Zambia by the late 1950s. African nationalism itself was energized by signals from London in the post–World War II period that the days of the British Empire were numbered (India's independence in 1947 was instrumental in this regard). Northern Rhodesia's nationalists were led by Harry Nkumbula and Kenneth Kaunda and their organization, the Northern Rhodesia African National Congress (NRANC), which was renamed the African National Congress (ANC) in 1953. In 1958, as nationalist agitation began to evoke harsh responses from the colonial regime, a split emerged between Nkumbula and Kaunda over how much to cooperate with colonial authorities. Kenneth Kaunda established a more radical faction, the Zambia African National Congress (ZANC), which was subsequently banned in 1959. Kaunda himself was imprisoned, but he emerged from prison in 1960 as the leader of the newly established United National Independence Party (UNIP).

Because of its history of relatively milder racial policies than other settler societies, domestic unrest in Zambia prompted constitutional negotiations, endorsed by Britain, rather than violence as in Southern Rhodesia. Constitutional negotiations took place in 1961–62, although the actual transfer to majority rule did not occur until more than two years later. As an interim step, an African majority was elected to the Northern Rhodesian Legislative Council in the 1962 elections. The changes at the national level were mirrored at the level of the federal government, which began to make minor concessions to blacks during this period. Northern Rhodesia achieved its independence on October 24, 1964, and the country became known officially as the Republic of Zambia. Prior to the official granting of independence, UNIP had won parliamentary elections by an overwhelming majority. The interim parliamentary system, which called for a prime minister, was scrapped in favor of a presidential system; UNIP leader Kenneth Kaunda became Zambia's first president, although the parliamentary legislature remained.

Zambia's First Republic (1964–72) was a nominally multiparty system, although UNIP clearly was the dominant party and Kaunda—with wide powers vested in the presidency and a compliant legislature—the dominant leader. In the first few years following independence, the ANC provided modest parliamentary opposition, but its 10 seats were largely ineffectual next to UNIP's 55 in the 65-seat National Assembly. Several other parties emerged during the First Republic, typically the result of factional splits within UNIP. Characteristic of one-party dominant regimes, however, UNIP became increasingly intolerant of competition over time. The fate of two opposition parties provide prominent examples: The United Party, which was established in 1966, was banned by the government in 1968; the United People's Party (UPP), which was set up in 1971, was banned only six months later.

The UPP was formed by Kaunda's former vice president, Simon Mwansa Kapwepwe, a prominent Bemba politician from Northern Province. The UPP posed particular problems for UNIP by attracting support from traditional UNIP strongholds in the Copperbelt and Northern Provinces, where ethnic Bemba form significant majorities. This tacit ethnic dimension, coupled with the emergence of interparty violence, gave Kaunda the pretext he needed to act on prior calls for the establishment of a one-party state in Zambia, thereby stamping out so-called disunity in the nation.

Concurrent with the banning of UPP in February 1972 and the arrest and detention of Kapwepwe and 123 leading members of the party, the UNIP cabinet announced its intention to establish a one-party participatory democracy. UNIP further consolidated its power by co-opting the leadership of the longtime opposition party, the ANC, and a constitutional amendment was passed in December 1972, which made Zambia a de jure one-party state. Kaunda then was sworn in as president of Zambia's Second Republic. A new constitution was passed in August 1973, permitting, among other things, competitive elections for the National Assembly, but only between UNIP party candidates and a plebiscite on Kaunda's rule every five years. The first elections under the single-party constitution were held in December 1973. The one-party state endured until 1991, when faced with economic collapse and rising domestic and international pressures, the UNIP parliament rescinded the one-party restriction at the president's behest, and Kaunda acquiesced to multiparty elections.

POLITICS AND ECONOMY

Economic Crisis and Political Transition

Today, Zambia is a multiparty democracy. Its system calls for a 150-seat parliament, the National Assembly, for which elections are held every five years between October and December. The president, who is directly elected by separate ballot, also serves for five years and enjoys substantial powers as head of state and head of government. The president is constitutionally limited to two terms. Zambia's democracy is imperfect, like many countries that have undergone recent transitions from long periods of authoritarianism, even relatively soft authoritarianism such as practiced by Kaunda. Yet the country has also made significant democratic advances since its 1991 transition. Indeed, despite its small size and largely uneventful postcolonial history, Zambia, represents something of a bellwether case for African democratization, not only in the 1990s but into the twenty-first century as well. Its transition from Kaunda's authoritarianism to the ostensibly democratic government that succeeded it was peaceful, fair, and internationally heralded. Much of the credit for this smooth transition goes to the Zambian people, of course, but Kaunda also deserves some plaudits as well. Although he fully expected to win, and wildly overestimated his popularity, he accepted defeat graciously.

Kaunda was compelled to agree to elections because of the economic collapse prevailing in the country and the social unrest, particularly in 1986, that he could no longer control. The catalyst for political change in Zambia lay in the collapse of the economy, which had been in steady decline for nearly two decades (shrinking at an average of 2.5 percent per year from 1975 to 1991).[3] Following independence in 1964, the Zambian government did little to diversify its export base, allowing copper to make up some 90 percent of the country's exports. This left Zambia particularly vulnerable to fluctuations in the global price of copper. It was not propitious that copper prices have seen a net overall decline, with some exceptions, since the mid-1970s. Zambia is also an oil-dependent, landlocked economy, factors that greatly increased cost of production, not only for copper but for any other goods produced by the economy as well. Finally, Kaunda's government—like many African governments that gained their independence in the 1960s—vigorously pursued what is known as statist development policies. Broadly socialist in its orientation, the Kaunda government embraced a development model that saw the state as the primary engine of economic development. Thus, beginning in 1967, the state became the major owner of capital in the country, acquiring majority shareholdings in existing firms and creating new ones. This activity was so dramatic that by the mid-1970s, some 80 percent of the Zambian economy was state controlled.

Such a course was understandable, given Zambians' need to catch up and historical discrimination against blacks; the state was among the only actors to play this role of "Zambianizing" the economy. Moreover, it was sustainable as long as copper retained high global demand and export revenues were robust. Once the copper economy collapsed, however, the Zambian economy collapsed along with it. The state was no longer able to meet its expenditures, especially on social welfare—schooling, health, subsidies—and was forced to borrow heavily from international lenders, including donor countries like Britain the United States and others, but chiefly from the World Bank and the International Monetary Fund (IMF or the Fund). Thus, in a span of less than 20 years, Zambia went from one of the richest, most promising countries in independent Africa to one of the most indebted and worst economies. By the late 1980s, it had accumulated an external debt of nearly $7 billion and could not meet its debt-service payments to the World Bank and the Fund.

Beginning in 1983, the Zambian government began the first of its Structural Adjustment Programs (SAPs) under the direction of the World Bank and the IMF, designed to restore external economic balances and growth. These failed,

A woman dries tobacco. Many farmers hoped exports like tobacco could reduce Zambia's economic dependence on copper. Courtesy of the author.

however, due to flaws in both design and implementation. Furthermore, the austere spending reductions called for by the World Bank and the Fund— including elimination of certain subsidies on the consumption of the staple food, maize meal—caused urban riots in 1986 that left more than 30 people dead, and President Kaunda was forced to halt the program.

This popular victory perhaps set the stage for Kaunda's later defeat at the polls and loss of the presidency and the government; it revealed that he and his administration had to be sensitive to popular opinion and protest. In a sense, this is a credit to the soft authoritarianism practiced by Kaunda. Although he was, in effect, a president for life and the preeminent power in the country, he was not a military ruler; he did not rule Zambia with brutal-ity, but he did stifle political opposition to his rule, especially after 1972.

On June 30, 1990, a rebel army lieutenant announced on state-owned radio that his soldiers had staged a coup and overthrown the UNIP government. The public reaction to the announcement was one of jubilation. Crowds took to the streets in Lusaka and elsewhere and hailed the putative overthrow of the government. The coup turned out to be more ephemeral than real; the soldiers had merely gained control of the broadcasting agency and had not secured the wider support of the armed forces, and the matter was settled quickly with their arrest. The episode shocked Kaunda, however, and revealed the depths of his unpopularity in the face of the country's economic stagnation and decline and unemployment. Indeed, combined with the food riots earlier and several days of riots in June 1990 that preceded the coup, these mass demonstrations laid bare the public disaffection with the economy, the lack of alternatives within the one-party structure, and, indeed, with Kaunda himself. Clearly, Kaunda had encouraged a cult of personality and sycophancy. Yet this also produces a tendency on the part of political elites to believe their own myth, thereby contributing to an inability to see the necessity for change in strategy and/or policy. To his credit, however, Kaunda clearly recognized it after the attempted coup in 1990 and began to allow the reintroduction of certain political freedoms in Zambia. These included the lifting of restrictions on the press and on freedom of speech and, eventually, the allowance of the formation of opposition parties (the discontinuation of the colonial era state of emergency that had granted the government broad powers of detention was only considered, however).

Civic groups in Zambia, meanwhile, were energized in this environment. In July 1991, a large group met at Lusaka's Garden House Hotel and formally launched the Movement for Multiparty Democracy (MMD), which almost instantly became the leading opposition party in the country. The leaders of the MMD were drawn from a broad cross section of Zambian society and included prominent leaders from Zambia's powerful labor union movement—often at odds with Kaunda in the past—the business community, academics, students, women's organizations, church and other civic leaders, and a number of disaffected former UNIP politicians and bureaucrats who had fallen out of favor with Kaunda in previous years.

When the national elections for president and parliament were held on October 31, 1991 (Zambia's first multiparty elections in more than 19 years), UNIP and MMD were joined in the contest by some seven additional, albeit minor, opposition parties. The MMD presidential candidate was the former leader of the Zambia Congress of Trade Unions, Frederick Chiluba, who as labor leader had long been a thorn in the side of Kaunda's government. Campaigning on the theme "The Hour Has Come," the MMD swept the national elections. The MMD victory was decisive, and its margin of victory surprised many observers, not least Kaunda, who lost the presidency to Chiluba by 73 percent to 27 percent. Kaunda's party fared even worse, gaining only 20 percent of the popular vote nationally and returning just 22 seats to parliament.

It is worth bearing in mind that Kaunda had been in office for 27 years and was the head of a one-party state for 19 years. In addition, given his role in the nationalist movement and Zambia's independence, he was widely seen as the Father of the Nation. Further, UNIP had been the only government in Zambia's history. If these features did not afford the party and president inexhaustible popularity (and they clearly did not, as evidenced by the 1991 poll results), they certainly conferred upon the party and president the formidable resources and networks of incumbency. Again, to his considerable credit, Kaunda graciously accepted defeat and turned over the reins of government to Chiluba and the MMD. In a continent that had known, to that time, few peaceful, civilian transfers of power, Zambia thus emerged as a model for the rest of the continent, at least in the eyes of many domestic and international observers. As noted later, however, these assessments proved overly optimistic and quite premature, as the decade that followed was marked by a series of fits and starts democratically as well as on the economic front.

In its platform, the MMD promised not only democracy for the country but also the revitalization of the economy that had seen years of decline under Kaunda's rule. Hence, MMD's victory was accompanied by a set of sweeping reforms aimed at revitalizing the moribund economy. Prominent among these was a reinstatement of the World Bank– and IMF-sponsored Structural Adjustment Program, SAP, which MMD embraced enthusiastically. Although the Zambian population clearly had suffered—and rioted—under previous iterations of the SAP during the Kaunda era, many were willing to give MMD the benefit of the doubt that new leadership, better governance, and modified liberalization policies were the keys to future national prosperity. For its part, the MMD was candid about the need for fiscal austerity, including the elimination of subsidies restored by Kaunda, and this may have helped the population prepare themselves for the dislocation to come.

The economic program thus called for a range of liberalization measures, which mainly emphasized the reduction or near elimination of the state role in the economy, which would thenceforth be guided by market forces. These included the elimination of exchange-rate controls and devaluation of the kwacha, the reduction of trade barriers, sharp reductions in government spending (including on the bureaucracy, consumer subsidies, social welfare, and state-owned industries), privatization of state-owned enterprises, and so on. Predictably, these changes resulted in extreme hardships for average Zambians, yet at the same time they failed to produce the widely hoped for economic revitalization. The region was hit by debilitating droughts in both 1992 and 1994–95 that caused major economic upheaval. In addition, critics of the SAP assailed both the World Bank and the IMF for imposing such austerity measures on Zambia and the MMD for accepting them. The international donor community and the World Bank and the IMF criticized the Chiluba administration for irregular and incomplete implementation of its proposals, thereby not fulfilling its end of the bargain. In fact, the recriminations directed at all parties appear to have been appropriate. Some of the policy prescriptions were themselves shortsighted and highly damaging—such as trade liberalization, for example—and the government was also guilty of corruption, mismanagement, and stalling when it benefited it politically.

Paradoxically, the MMD was able to exploit the power and resources of the state in much the same way, and arguably worse, than had UNIP and Kaunda. Indeed, given the economic precipice on which Zambia found itself in the 1990s, the corrupt activities of the Chiluba regime had far-reaching consequences. Democracy was shallow in the period, despite the promise of the 1991 elections. Critically, institutional change—including limits on the power of the presidency, for example—was not part of the 1991 transition, and Chiluba used the power of his office to intimidate, marginalize, and co-opt his opponents. Decision-making lacked transparency and was the preserve of a small clique surrounding the president without consultation with other bodies or society. The parliament, in which MMD held 128 of 150 seats after 1991, was no less pliant than under Kaunda. In addition, Chiluba quickly installed MMD sympathizers to the courts. Thus, any semblance of balance of power between branches of government was lost.

On the other hand, however, there clearly were some important democratic gains after 1991. Civil society, which had become so mobilized in the effort to oust Kaunda, remained something of a political watchdog, and various nongovernmental organizations (NGOs) proliferated that spoke out frequently against perceived government transgressions and poor policies. The independent press was equally vigilant. Most prominently, the privately owned *Weekly Post* newspaper (which later became a daily, *The Post*) constantly railed against the MMD, often at great personal risk to the paper's editors and writers. It is important to point out, however, that in spite of their important role, these groups were able to affect MMD direction only at the margins for the most part. In short, the early 1990s was something of a free-for-all riddled with paradoxes. Some of the restrictions of the Kaunda era had been eliminated, but, at the same time, the new democratic government engaged in corruption of unprecedented magnitude and with impunity. More public criticism was heard, but it was largely ignored as the wider populace lacked the means to affect policy; MMD members of parliament (MPs), who dominated parliament, were responsible less to their constituencies than to their leaders in the ruling party. In such a system, maverick politicians are a rarity because loyalty to the party is rewarded by political advancement.

The government did respond to those critics it saw as most threatening, however, although the instruments of response were intimidation and imprisonment. Prominently among those who were targeted by the MMD in this period were the outspoken and popular editor of *The Post* newspaper and, later, Kaunda himself and certain opposition politicians. Although political parties proliferated in the period, many turned out to be merely personal vehicles of their founders with few if any followers. As a result, Zambia under the MMD became a de facto one-party state.

Socially and economically, the vast majority of Zambians continued to suffer in the 1990s. As MMD politicians profited, most Zambians grew rapidly poorer as the number of people living in poverty stood at more than 86 percent. The economic reform program generated few benefits. Unpredictable droughts forced Zambia to rely on substantial food aid two out of the first five years of the Second Republic. In addition, AIDS cases began to accelerate markedly in Zambia, as they did throughout Africa, creating massive social dislocation and a national crisis in manpower, cost, healthcare, and economy. (HIV-AIDS has reached epidemic proportions in Zambia, infecting some 19 percent of the adult population, a topic revisited in chapter 6.)

In 1996, Zambia held its second election since the return of the multiparty system. Whereas the euphoria surrounding the 1991 transition might have led some to predict that by 1996 Zambia would be well on its way to democratic consolidation, in fact it was headed the opposite direction. Indeed, instead of democratic consolidation, the November 1996 elections arguably marked the nadir of Zambian politics in nearly four decades of independence.

Despite the fact that it still maintained measurable public support (partly because of the absence of truly credible alternatives among the opposition), MMD nevertheless was fearful that it might face substantial electoral losses in 1996. Former president Kaunda had made an improbable comeback and was prepared to challenge Chiluba for the presidency. Hence, the MMD manipulated the constitution by pushing through constitutional reforms in May 1996 that deliberately barred Kaunda from running for president. The international community condemned the action, but Chiluba refused to capitulate. He even ordered several of Kaunda's UNIP colleagues jailed on trumped-up charges of coup-plotting.

In addition to its constitutional machinations, the MMD also resorted to a number of other antidemocratic measures to retain its hold on power. For example, it orchestrated a national voter registration drive that was widely seen as secretive and corrupt. It clamped down viciously on the independent press and leading members of rival parties, including UNIP. In response to the government's actions, many opposition parties called for a boycott of the November elections. Most of the international community, including groups like the United States–based Carter Center, refused to participate as election observers, fearing that their presence would lend legitimacy to the process. As it turned out, UNIP candidates did withdraw, but some opposition parties opted to participate. Other candidates ran for parliament as independents. In this highly incendiary and unbalanced electoral environment, non-MMD candidates won only 19 seats in the National Assembly, including 10 independents.

MMD's abuse of power, both during and before the election, as well as its inability to revive the economy left Zambians more depressed than ever, and this was reflected in the abysmal turnout for the election: Only around 25 percent of eligible voters bothered to come to the polls. Hence, what might have been the triumph of democracy in Zambia—once deemed Africa's model—appeared instead to be the twilight of democracy.

Nonetheless, the fact that growth and democracy may come in fits and starts need not negate the chances of their eventual entrenchment in the fabric of African politics and society.[4] Indeed, despite its considerable democratic setbacks, some important basic liberties were won in Zambia's transition that became entrenched, even by the 1996 elections. Civil society was emboldened, resulting in active and vocal associations and a critical free press. Although disorganized, a plethora of parties came into existence.

The 2001 Elections and Beyond

Although the picture we have painted of Zambia in the 1990s is indeed a grim one, Zambians are incredibly resourceful and resilient people. In early 2001, it looked like it was going to get much worse politically and, by extension, socioeconomically. Anxious to maintain access to the spoils of office, President Chiluba strongly hinted in early 2001 that he would attempt to stand again for the presidency in the elections later that year. Although barred by the constitution from a third term, President Chiluba, who had successfully steered the rewriting of the constitution in 1996, was undeterred. It was widely expected that Chiluba would be successful, ramming through the necessary constitutional amendments, easily convincing an obsequious party, and overcoming a weak opposition in parliament.

Just when it appeared that Zambia would be consigned to the category of failed democratic experiments, something quite unexpected happened. Zambia's civil society rose up and rejected Chiluba's bid for to seek a third term by altering the constitution (it is widely assumed that Chiluba and MMD would have resorted to any means to secure election victory). Largely ignored for a decade, these downtrodden and too often abused members of Zambia's body politic—churches, lawyers, NGOs, business, labor, students, and others—again were stirred to action. They took to the streets in a massive "No Third Term" campaign. They organized seminars and assembled a formidable coalition of civic groups and politicians. The anti–Third Term movement was so successful that it even managed to convince 22 sitting members of Chiluba's own cabinet that the jig was up. Many parliamentarians also joined in by stating that they would not support any proposed change to the constitutional clause on term limits. Faced with massive public pressure and insurrection within his own party, Chiluba backed down.

Unable to run himself, Chiluba anointed Levy Mwanawasa, a lawyer and his onetime vice president (1991–93), as the MMD's presidential candidate and Chiluba's heir apparent. It was widely believed that Chiluba would simply rule from the background and saw Mwanawasa as a puppet. First, however, Mwanawasa and MMD had to get past a divided but newly energized political opposition. A total of 11 parties fielded candidates for the presidential contest, and 17 fielded candidates for the parliamentary election (a number of people also ran as independents). Among the most formidable opposition parties at this time was the United Party for National Development (UPND), which had been launched in December 1998 by prominent Tonga businessman Anderson Mazoka and had by early 2001 captured a handful of seats in parliament through interim elections.

In the event, Mwanawasa defeated his nearest challenger, Mazoka, by 28 percent to 26 percent of the vote, the rest being split among the remaining candidates. In the parliamentary election, MMD captured 27.4 percent (69 seats) to UPND's 23.3 percent (49 seats), and five other parties shared the remainder. International observer groups such as those led by the Carter Center and the European Union delegation condemned the result, claiming that the electoral process had not been free and fair. It was a credit to Zambians that they resorted to legal channels rather than violence to contest the controversial MMD victory. It was thus under a political and legal cloud that Mwanawasa took office on January 2, 2002.

Mwanawasa, however, proved to be a surprise, and a mostly pleasant one at that, particularly following the widespread corruption and macroeconomic mismanagement that obtained under the Chiluba government. President Mwanawasa demonstrated that he was not beholden to his benefactor Chiluba. Indeed, Mwanawasa instituted a vigorous program to target official corruption under his predecessor. Even Chiluba himself saw his immunity lifted by the parliament in July 2002 at the urging of Mwanawasa and amidst continued public pressure. Chiluba's trial began in December 2003. Although there was a great deal of circumstantial evidence against the former president, it was not clear that he would be convicted. Witness cooperation had been difficult to garner (Chiluba remained a very powerful actor in his own right), and much of the corrupt activities that occurred during his rule were orchestrated by underlings. The difficulty of a conviction was further revealed with a reduction in the number of charges against the former president in 2004.

Nevertheless, the prosecution of Chiluba was a major turning point, not only in Zambia but in Africa as a whole. It introduced into the political realm the seeds of a new culture of civic responsibility and checks on power that augured well for the country's future.

Economically, Zambia remained extremely poor, although between 2001 and 2005 the economy registered impressive growth. President Mwanawasa's first term proved him somewhat erratic politically but a reasonable steward of the economy, which certainly benefited by favorable copper prices, donor largesse, and measurable (and potentially total) debt reductions.[5] All these trends must continue if Zambia is to improve the welfare of its nearly 11 million citizens.

NOTES

1. As in most Bantu languages, both the people (ethnic groups) and languages they speak have specific prefixes that indicate whether one is referring to language (siLozi, iciBemba), a single individual (mlozi), the entire group (Batonga), and so on. For the purpose of clarity, this book mainly uses the same root (e.g., Bemba) to describe all three categories. If the specific use of the African word is not obvious from the context, it is coupled with the English noun (e.g., the Bemba language).

2. Gertzel, "Introduction: The Making of the One-Party State," p 10.

3. Rakner, *Political and Economic Liberalisation in Zambia, 1990–2001,* 54, 66.

4. Fomunyoh, "Democratization in Fits and Starts," 37–50.

5. Under the World Bank's enhanced Heavily Indebted Poor Countries (HIPC) Initiative, Zambia qualified for $3.9 billion in debt relief in 2001 and a comparable amount in early 2006.

2

Religion and Worldview

Zambia is a religiously plural environment that includes both world religions, such as Christianity, Islam, and Hinduism, as well as traditional practices. The vast majority of its population, however, practices various denominations of Christianity. Christianity arrived in the country in the mid-nineteenth century but did not establish a solid foothold in the country until the early twentieth century as missionary activity proliferated in conjunction with the establishment of colonial control over the territory. Christianity now claims more than three-quarters of the population as adherents, and though many of the traditional beliefs survive (and may coexist with Christian beliefs), surely the infusion of Western and specifically Christian religious practice impacted the ways in which Zambians view the world. *Webster's New World Dictionary, Third College Edition* defines *worldview* as "a comprehensive, especially personal, philosophy or conception of the world and of human life." As such, it is difficult to take what is, at bottom, an intensely personal characteristic and apply it to an entire population of more than 10 million people. After all, the worldview of Zambians, as of people anywhere, is influenced by their personal experiences, memories, circumstances, as well as their religious or spiritual convictions. Thus, wealth, education, access to resources, and the like all impact how any individual conceives of the world. Nevertheless, acknowledging that the notion of worldview cannot easily be assigned to an entire country, it is possible to identify a few characteristics that influence life—and lives, individually and collectively—in Zambia and, therefore, serve to shape people's perspectives (even if not all those in the country). Among these, religion is one of the most important; therefore, religion and worldview are examined together here.

In the pre-Christian, precolonial period, the worldview of most people who lived in what is now Zambia was affected by their surroundings: their relationships with neighbors and with nature. This, in turn, influenced their spirituality and how they conceived of God, which also impacted their relationships, in a kind of virtuous circle. Thus, it could be said that religion and worldview were inextricably linked. In the pre-Christian period, the notion of worldview would have been much more narrowly conceived in the literal sense. For one, the known world was far smaller in scope, familiarity being limited to neighboring groups, some of whom were regarded as vassals, others as enemies. Religion was undergirded by spirituality that saw God in nature and celebrated the role and importance of one's ancestors. Christianity brought a different notion of religion, more formal and institutionalized, and thus changed the nature of the average Zambian's relationship with his creator and with families and neighbors. For many, spirituality—religion—therefore became something that was practiced at church. The missionaries created adherents, whereas in the past, religion was far more pervasive. Interestingly, some contemporary Christian practices may be more consistent with the latter, as discussed later in the chapter.

Since the advent of Christianity, and especially its emergence as the dominant national religion by the time of independence, Zambia has seen the rise of a worldview affected not only by Western religions but by Western economic, political, and cultural practices as well. In other words, postcolonial Zambia existed and exists in a far more globalized environment and therefore is subject to many more influences—secular and nonsecular—than was the case even a few years before. This global exposure has increased exponentially in the years since independence in 1964. Moreover, the rise of more evangelical strands of Christianity in contemporary Zambia has altered this worldview still further, at least to the growing number of Zambians who adhere to these practices. Thus, today, although the religion is mainly Christian, the worldview is a combination of modernism and nature-rooted spiritualism, communalism, and optimism. Today, Zambia's worldview is also defined by its well-earned peace-loving reputation, a collective interest in living in harmony with each other and internationally. Certainly, some of the components of worldview might be described as cultural traits that span both the pre-Christian and contemporary periods—family centeredness, adaptability, cohesiveness—although it would be wrong to suggest that these characteristics are immutable ones. Indeed, whether individual or collective, worldview is not necessarily fixed, and various forces, including economic uncertainty,

AIDS and other diseases, and widespread poverty, clearly impact most Zambians' perspective.

History of Religious Practices in Zambia

As in much of sub-Saharan Africa, Zambian peoples practiced a range of traditional religions and adhered to an array of religious beliefs before the coming of Christianity in the late nineteenth century. Even after the arrival of Christian missionaries on a measurable scale, beginning in the late 1880s, the majority of Zambian communities continued to adhere to traditional practices. Indeed, Christianity did not take root in most cultures until well into the twentieth century. It was only after the entrenchment of the colonial state after the turn of the century and the widespread establishment of permanent missions by the 1920s that most Zambians converted to or adopted Christianity as a religion. Importantly, many continued to maintain, at least initially, a number of traditional beliefs alongside their new Christian faiths, and many of these traditional beliefs and practices continue to influence behavior and cultural norms. Today, Zambians are well represented in all of the major Christian denominations, although evangelical churches, many not affiliated with a particular Christian faith tradition, are also on the rise. Christianity plays a prominent role in everyday life.

Zambia is overwhelmingly (more than 75 percent, though precise figures are not available) Christian, although other religions maintain a limited presence, including Islam and Hinduism, particularly among members of the populace who are of South Asian origin. Moreover, traditional practices still claim many adherents in remote areas, though these practices can coexist even within individuals who might otherwise describe themselves as Christian; relatively few Zambians practice traditional beliefs exclusively in the contemporary era. (Note that this contributes to the variation in estimates of the Christian population, which range from 72 percent to 90 percent.) This appears to be quite different from a number of other countries in the subregion, including Zimbabwe and Kenya, where traditional practices continue in many areas largely unfettered by the encroachments of so-called modern religions.

Indigenous Religions and Religious Practices

Like most African countries, a deep spirituality pervades Zambian culture. As the corporeal existence of Zambians is obviously strenuous and difficult, spirituality is guided by a supernatural force or forces that influence daily life. Hence, God/nature, one's ancestors, evil, and so on pervade the culture.

Although aspects of this have been diminished with the spread of Western norms and behaviors, most Zambians still have a sense that little in life happens by chance.

In the precolonial era, some of this spirituality bore resemblance to monotheistic world religions. For example, even in the pre-Christian era, most Zambians believed in a creator, a High God, referred to by a range of names—Nyambe in Lozi, Nzambi in the western regions, Mulungu in Nyanja, Leza in Tonga, or Lesa in the Bemba tongue, for example—responsible for creating the earthly and spiritual realms.[1] This High God/deity was not believed to play an active role in the everyday life of human beings, however. Instead, this space was occupied by the spirit realm. In this sense, traditional practices were not monotheistic in that there were a number of spirit or intermediate realms occupied by different types of spirits: ancestral, nature, individual. Although these were not worshipped per se, spirits in this intermediate realm were believed to control everything from the weather to pestilence to the availability of food to death and disease. Within this spiritual realm, the ancestors were particularly important to the various ethnicities. Although the ancestors occupy a milieu (very) roughly comparable to saints in other faith traditions, they should not be considered tantamount to guardian angels, however. Indeed, whereas the spirits of the ancestors could bring luck and success, if treated with the proper reverence, failure to properly appease them could result in bad luck and misfortune.

So-called nature spirits were also important. Among the Bemba, for example, the belief in the High God and ancestral spirits was "supplemented by beliefs in spirits called *ngulu*. These were not forces of nature, rather they represented the land in which they had their abodes. *Ngulu* inhabited strange natural features, such as rocks or waterfalls, where they received offerings from hereditary priests. They were not believed to be spirits of dead people, but they had names which were also given to people, and they were sometimes thought of as early inhabitants of their various countries."[2] Finally, individual spirits were seen as governing personal behavior.

At bottom, in addition to differing views on whom or what is God, Zambian traditional practices also deviated from Western conceptions of Heaven and earth as two rather distinct spaces. In many of the Zambian traditions, the real, observable world (the visible realm) and spirit realms were seen as interacting with one another rather than clearly delineated. Similarly, the world of the living and that of the dead lacked the neat separation they enjoy in the Western conception.

WITCHCRAFT

Traditional belief systems also accommodate the existence of witchcraft, which is thought to occur still in many communities, though it is widely condemned. If the spirit realms discussed previously can be considered mainly positive interpretations of the supernatural, witchcraft, which is regarded as distinct from the ancestors and spirits, carries a largely negative connotation. Many Zambians believe that witchcraft is practiced; however, witchcraft itself is not so much a belief system, per se, as it is a term associated with bad or at least suspicious behavior or inexplicable phenomena. In other words, behavior or events that cannot be explained through normal means often attracts the label of witchcraft; it is, of course, highly subjective. Thus, for example, if an individual suffered from an unexplained run of bad luck—or, conversely, having too much good luck—witchcraft was often suspected. These notions live on in contemporary perceptions and practices of alleged witchcraft.

In Western scholarship, much has been made of the issue of witchcraft in Africa. Some writers even go so far as to use the existence of witchcraft to denigrate Africa as premodern or backward, thereby branding Africa and Africans as incapable of change and of adjustment to modern Western practices, including democracy, capitalism, and so on.[3] Certainly, the practice or allegations of witchcraft in Africa, a subject that attracts a great deal of research interest, particularly from anthropologists, generates considerable misunderstanding for most Western popular audiences. Even the word *witchcraft* is so steeped in Westernism as to conjure up images of devilry, covens, and the Salem, Massachusetts, witch trials of the seventeenth century. Thus, in Western parlance, the notion or practice of witchcraft almost universally carries a negative connotation. In many African cultures it is often negative as well, and in the most extreme instances the accusation of witchcraft can bring ostracism or even death. At the same time, however, the idea of witchcraft is more nuanced than in the West. This is precisely why most anthropologists, while continuing to employ the terminology, recognize that witchcraft itself is a problematic term—the result of imprecise translations into English or French in particular—that actually can encompass African forms of magic, the occult, and, in some respects, aspects of traditional religious practices. Historically, therefore, witchcraft could have both good and bad forms, and anthropologists themselves acknowledge that contemporary study of witchcraft, per se, can contribute to further so-called exoticizing of Africa.

If further exoticizing of Africa is the consequence, however unintended, it has not stopped anthropologists from researching the subject. Indeed, some suggest that in Zambia and in the rest of Africa people not only continue to practice witchcraft but it is also resurgent—in politics, culture, and even religion—as a means of coping with modernity or, more specifically, globalization. Therefore, it is regarded, paradoxically, as both premodern or traditional and new.[4] It is not clear that there is any perceptible resurgence of witchcraft in Zambia; however, it does appear that witchcraft itself has been modernized in the sense that it is deployed today in ways that reflect contemporary life and social and political forces.

A prominent illustration of this phenomenon is the case of Katele Kalumba, the former finance minister and onetime foreign minister. Accused of theft of state assets while serving in the Frederick Chiluba government, Kalumba led police on a three-month manhunt before he was finally arrested in January 2003. Some policemen accused Kalumba of resorting to witch-craft, which enabled him to know the whereabouts of his police trackers and thereby elude capture for such a long time. The police reported that when they finally caught up with Kalumba, he was wearing charms and carrying a fetish and other items that, it was said, allowed him to be invisible. Yet in an illustration of the nuanced role and character of witchcraft, according to some reports, the police used good witchcraft and the assistance of a witch doctor to locate him.

On the one hand, the police accused Kalumba—an educated, cosmopolitan, former senior minister—of practicing witchcraft, which they publicly denounced as arcane, desperate, and even ridiculous. In so doing, their inten-tions were twofold: the first was to make him an object of scorn and derision, or worse—the frequent fate of purported witches; the second intention was to mock this putative sophisticate as thoroughly unmodern. On the other hand, however, it seems the police apparently felt comfortable using witch-craft ostensibly to combat it (or at least its alleged practitioner, in this case, Kalumba). In short, the police sought to both ridicule and uphold the exis-tence of witchcraft simultaneously. Even a committed cultural relativist might describe this scenario, particularly the behavior of the police, as bizarre.

CHRISTIANITY

Pre-Christian beliefs in a High God, in other intermediaries, such as ances-tors, and even in the presence of good and evil represented within witchcraft practices undergirded Zambian spirituality. Certainly this pre-Christian spirituality of Zambian peoples in many ways infuses their contemporary beliefs. A linguistic thread also ties the eras together, as Lesa, Leza, and other indigenous names for the High God are today used to refer to the God of the Christian Bible. The highly spiritual nature of Zambian society also helps to explain the zeal and relative ease with which the vast majority of Zambians came to embrace Christianity and in a relatively short span of time.

Although European Christians, principally Portuguese explorers, had had some contact with Zambian peoples as early as the fifteenth century, the origins of widespread and sustained interaction between Zambia and Christianity date to the mid-nineteenth century. Among the first to introduce Christianity to Zambia was the famed Scottish missionary and explorer Dr. David Livingstone, who first traveled to the region via South Africa in 1851. Livingstone was at least as interested in exploration as he was in spreading the Gospel, and his legacy reflects the former. Yet after Livingstone's death in 1874, near Lake Bangwelu in the border region with what is today Tanzania, the tales of his exploits helped give rise to extensive missionary activity as well as the expansion of colonialism. Livingstone himself was a Scots Presbyterian, and that denomination became particularly influential in eastern Zambia and Malawi, where he also traveled extensively. Subsequent missionary activity included Roman Catholics, Anglicans, and Baptist denominations. Among the first permanent missions was established by the London Missionary Society (LMS), which set up a mission among the Mambwe in 1887 and the Lungu in 1889, although these initial attempts had only limited success at spreading the Gospel.

Notwithstanding the LMS's lack of early results, missionary work to convert Africans to Christianity proceeded most rapidly among the Bemba and Lozi peoples, which began to have an impact as early as the 1890s. Roughly speaking, Protestantism gained a greater foothold in the western part of the country and Roman Catholicism in the east. For example, French Protestants had established a mission at Sefula, a Lozi town, in 1886. Although the Lozi king, Lewanika, later brought in black South African missionaries from the (African American) AME Church in 1904–5, this effort failed financially.[5] The French were also active in eastern Zambia, where French missionaries of the Roman Catholic White Fathers founded a mission among the Mambwe people in 1891. A mission in Bembaland was founded in 1895 as Roman Catholicism became a major influence in what is now Northern Province.

Of course, Christianity served a dual purpose in Africa: to save savage, heathen Africa, spiritually as well as open it commercially. Whereas the enthusiasm of white European missionaries (whose ranks were later joined by some African Americans as well as Africans) for their ecclesiastical objectives was probably genuine in most cases, there is little question that these religious actors helped usher in the colonial era. Indeed, upon his return to England in 1856 following his initial trip to the Zambia region, even Livingstone announced to an audience at Cambridge that "I go back to Africa to try to make a path for commerce and Christianity." Thus, the two were linked even by perhaps the foremost Christian missionary-cum-explorer of the day. Directly and indirectly, Christianity also helped diminish resistance to colonialism. Although it is important not to overstate the role of Christianity in pacifying Zambian peoples—the foundations of colonialism were laid as much with European guns as with Bibles—Christianity nonetheless served, to paraphrase Karl Marx, as the "opiate of the masses" by convincing many

Africans to accept their lot on earth, however discriminated against they were, or became, in colonial society; earthly hardship was countered by the promise of salvation in the hereafter. Interestingly, the vastly different attitudes toward materialism and wealth accumulation that characterize many of the modern fundamentalist Protestant churches doubtlessly would have proved far less compatible with colonialism.

At the same time, however, the work of the missions laid much of the groundwork for Zambia's future in ways both intended and unintended. As discussed in chapter 3, missionary activity eventually included translation of the Bible into local tongues. Whereas this clearly facilitated the indoctrination of many into the faith, it was also in many respects a departure from the ordinary colonial model. After all, despite the fact that Christianity and commerce came to all of Africa as two sides of the same coin, commerce—and its attendant imperialism and the exploitation of African people and resources—quickly became the dominant force in European-African relations. Yet Christianity became a tool of communication—both in terms of speaking the same language of Christ and his teachings as well as literally, because missionary schools often provided the first formal educational opportunities for Africans to learn a European language, typically English.

In Zambia, Africans were seen principally as a source of labor for the mining and commercial agricultural activities that underpinned the colonial economy. Teaching Africans to read and write, therefore, was not necessarily conducive to the creation of a semiskilled, wage-based economy; in fact, in some respects it was antithetical to it. Nonetheless, the churches played an instrumental role in education. They built schools and educated a class of Zambians who became important leaders. Many Africans who were beneficiaries of mission education themselves became teachers, and many of these teachers, in turn, came to play prominent roles in the nationalist and independence movements in Zambia. African elites such as Simon Kapwepwe and future President Kenneth Kaunda were educated at Lubwa, a mission in Northern Province established by Kaunda's father, David, himself a missionary from neighboring Malawi. This mission-educated elite, therefore, became leaders of the liberation movements of the 1950s that eventually sought, and won, Zambian independence.

CONTEMPORARY CHURCHES IN ZAMBIA

Consistent with Roman Catholicism's early foothold in Zambia, particularly among the numerically dominant Bemba people, Catholics today remain the largest single denomination in Zambia, representing approximately one-third of all Christians. This is followed by other mainline Protestant denominations, such as the Anglican Church. Other active denominations include the Seventh-Day Adventists and the Jehovah's Witnesses, which have had for nearly a century a strong base in Luapula Province and which clashed repeatedly with the Kaunda government. The charismatic Protestant churches, most of which are nondenominational, are the fastest growing. These churches have established a substantial following not only in Zambia but all over sub-Saharan Africa. Importantly, given Christian predominance in the country, those drawn to the evangelical churches represent a net loss of members for other traditions.

The appeal of these new churches is manifold. For example, although more and more traditional Christian churches have incorporated singing and dancing far more akin to African traditional rhythms than the standard Western hymnal, the charismatic evangelical churches tend to incorporate a degree of singing and dancing in the audience, combined with a potent sermon delivered with fiery oratory, that results in a livelier service. Because many young Zambians no longer feel beholden to the faith traditions of their parents (much as they had deserted the pre-Christian beliefs of their own forebears), the congregants tend to be younger as well. They also employ a number of traditional elements: singing, dancing, and praise-singing that

A Catholic seminarian leads drummers and members of the choir during a wedding ceremony. Courtesy of the author.

characterize indigenous belief traditions. (Interestingly, even the Roman Catholic liturgy has incorporated singing, drumming, and dancing into church services, but this is usually limited to the choir and other participants, rather than the wider congregation.)

Despite their appeal to certain Zambian musical and cultural traditions, the principal model for the evangelical movement is American. In fact, U.S. televangelists, such as Billy Graham, Benny Hinn, T. D. Jakes, and others, enjoy enormous popularity in Zambia, and their sermons are frequently broadcast on Zambian television, ZNBC. One uniquely U.S. import, or at least influence, is the rise of so-called megachurches in this charismatic community. Among the emergent megachurches is the giant Bread of Life Church, a Baptist institution that in 2005 sought to break ground on a proposed Blessing Centre that would incorporate a gigantic 10,000-person sanctuary, a Bible school, and a primary school. The new facility also planned three studios to facilitate TV and radio ministry, signaling that U.S.-style televangelism has gained considerable popularity in Zambia. Indeed, as discussed in chapter 3, Christian-based radio stations have already established a foothold, among them Radio Christian Voice, which broadcasts Christian music and programming (some by satellite, originating in the United Kingdom Voice station) in Lusaka and the Copperbelt, and Yasane Radio, a Catholic-based station.

On the whole, the charismatic and fundamentalist churches are also far more accommodating of capitalism and tolerant of wealth and conspicuous consumption, which is another similarity to their U.S. counterparts. Indeed, much of the entrepreneurial class that emerged commensurate with economic liberalization in the 1990s has found a home in this movement, where their attainments tend to be celebrated rather than criticized. Not surprisingly, recent years have seen a growing degree of overlap between politics and public expressions of Christian faith, if not necessarily fundamentalism.

The evangelical movement gained a prominent representative when self-professed born-again Christian Frederick Chiluba was elected president in 1991. Chiluba declared Zambia a Christian nation shortly after his election and led a controversial but ultimately successful initiative to have this enshrined in the preamble to the constitution in 1996. Predictably, this both worried and offended many Zambians, including those of other faiths, as well as those who sought to promote religious pluralism and tolerance and regarded such a declaration as both unnecessary and divisive. Moreover, Chiluba's reported marital infidelities, massive corruption (for which he faced legal charges in 2003), and abuse of power were decidedly un-Christian behaviors, hence most observers both inside and outside Zambia, saw the Christian-nation effort as a rather cynical one intended to manipulate public opinion solely for political gain. Fortunately, the heralding of Zambia as a Christian nation had little negative impact on non-Christian populations. It was a political ploy, but the symbolism was nonetheless important for its potential divisiveness.

If Chiluba used religion for cynical political gain, Zambian evangelical preacher Pastor Nevers Mumba—whose style mirrored that of the U.S. televangelists—appeared to enter politics for the purpose of advancing a more genuine Christian agenda. Increasingly outspoken on political matters, Pastor Mumba transformed his religious organization, the National Christian Coalition, into a political party, the National Citizens' Coalition (NCC), under whose aegis he contested the presidency in 2001. Although Mumba lost decisively, this should not necessarily be regarded as a referendum on the role of religion in political life. Indeed, in 2002 Mumba was appointed national vice president by President Levy Mwanawasa, despite having no political experience, and he served in that post until 2004. Moreover, the churches have continued to play an important role in the political sphere: for example, working collectively as part of the Oasis Forum, the civil society organization that spearheaded the successful "No Third Term" campaign against President Chiluba in 2001. Subsequently, the leading Christian churches, as well as the Evangelical Federation of Zambia, were instrumental in exposing the malfeasance of the Chiluba administration (1991–2001) and demanding public accountability.

THE ISLAMIC MINORITY

Although Muslims represent only about 1 percent of the populace, they have a prominent position in society, especially in the cities of Lusaka and Livingstone. Most of Zambia's small Muslim minority hails from the Indian subcontinent; Indians were brought to Africa by the British to serve as a merchant class in the colonial period. Over time, their commercial interests grew considerably, and this class continued to prosper after colonialism. In general, the Indian Muslim community is quite cohesive, and although not exactly insular, as is the case with similar minority populations in Kenya and Tanzania, for example, the community's mosques, places of business, and residences are often found in close proximity. One prominent example of this is Luburma/Madras and the adjacent Kamwala neighborhood in Lusaka, which in addition to being a thriving commercial center also boasts one of Zambia's largest and most established mosques.

Other Muslims are of Arab or Middle Eastern descent and also form an intermediary economic class. Black Muslims in Zambia are generally converts to the religion or immigrants from West Africa. Interestingly, whereas non-black Muslims are frequently wealthy, black Muslims are often considered of lower social class. Occasionally, they are referred to derisively as Senegalese *(Msene),* whether or not they hail from Senegal; the Senegalese were among the first black Muslims to come to Zambia in any appreciable numbers, and the name stuck to those who followed.

Importantly, whereas the 1996 Christian-nation declaration was justifiably controversial, in fact, the paucity of non-Christians in the country means that the country actually is Christian, for all intents and purposes. Conflict between Christians and Muslims, however, such as that which occurs regularly in more closely divided societies, like Nigeria, is rare. Moreover, where Christian-Muslim conflict does occur, it is much more likely to be about economic issues, and religious differences are merely coincidental. For example, Black Zambians and those of Indian descent (who may happen to be Muslim, or Hindu, for that matter) have clashed occasionally over the years; however, this has had more to do with perceived discrimination and social practices than religious ones. By and large, the different faith communities live harmoniously with one another.

Current President Mwanawasa even went so far in 2004 as to criticize the profile of Muslims in Zambia as being too low. Reaching out to the Muslim population on a visit to the Makeni Islamic Centre in Lusaka, he implored them to participate more actively in politics. He praised the work of the Makeni Muslim Society, which runs a medical clinic that services more than 4,000 patients per month and primary, secondary, and vocational schools around Zambia. In fact, the president's reputation for religious tolerance earned him the support of the Kabwe Muslim Association, which instructed its members to vote for Mwanawasa and the ruling Movement for Multiparty Democracy (MMD) in the 2006 presidential elections. Although insignificant from an electoral standpoint, such an endorsement carries important symbolism. For its part, the larger Islamic Council of Zambia (ICZ) generally endorsed Mwanawasa's appeal for greater Muslim participation in the political process, though it adopted a nonpartisan stance; the ICZ merely called on its membership to register to vote, cast ballots wisely, and stand as candidates in the election.

HINDU AND OTHER MINORITY RELIGIONS

Although the majority of Zambians of Indian descent are Muslim, a sizable percentage are Hindu. Like their Muslim counterparts, longtime resident Zambian Hindus were brought to Africa by the British during the colonial period to serve as a merchant class. Today, Hindus form a relatively small and cohesive community residing in towns across the country, although most are concentrated in Lusaka, Copperbelt, and Southern Provinces, chiefly in the commercial centers of Lusaka, Ndola, and Livingstone. Nationally, Hindu Hall in Lusaka is the most prominent religious and communal facility, whereas temples and branches of the Hindu Association of Zambia are located in many municipalities, including Ndola, and smaller towns like Kafue. The Hindu Temple in the small Southern Province city of Monze, for example, became a cultural center for Indians in that area.

Although at times tensions based on religious prejudice and class rivalry have boiled over in incidents of violence, Hindu Zambians actively and positively participate in economic and political matters. In 1996, however, three days of rioting and looting occurred in Livingstone in which shops owned by the city's affluent Hindu (and Muslim) community were explicitly targeted. Yet wealthy Hindu Zambians have contributed generously to famine-relief efforts, among other charitable efforts, and have played a role in the prodemocracy movement. Moreover, in the same year the anti-Asian violence took place in Livingstone, Dipak Patel, then a cabinet minister in the Chiluba government, quit the MMD and ran for parliament as an independent. Patel, who is both Hindu and of Indian descent, defeated a black, Christian MMD candidate to capture the Lusaka Central constituency.[6] Patel was an outspoken critic of the second Chiluba administration and was repeatedly harassed by the president's men. Nonetheless, he was named minister of commerce, trade and industry in the Mwanawasa government, which itself split with Chiluba.

In the postcolonial era, ethnoreligious ties to the Indian subcontinent that contributed to Hindu Zambians' commercial success have served to facilitate important political and economic cooperation between Zambia and India. In 2003, Zambia signed trade-cooperation agreements with India, and First Lady Maureen Mwanawasa hosted a cultural exchange of Indian dancers in Lusaka's Hindu Hall. In the following year, Hindu dancers played a role in the celebration of the 40th anniversary of Zambia's independence.

Although most Zambian Jewry departed the country in the 1960s, a small Jewish community continues to reside in Zambia, concentrated mainly around Lusaka. Zambian Jews have extremely diverse roots that date to the late nineteenth century when the first Jewish settlers arrived and established themselves as traders and farmers. Over the years, these Yiddish-speaking Jews were joined by Ladino speakers from the former Ottoman Empire as well as Anglophones from South Africa, England, and Ireland. Immigration continued through the close of World War II when mainly German-speaking Holocaust survivors arrived in the country. Today, only a relative handful of Jews remain, although they, too, have played prominent roles in Zambian commerce and politics, including the appointment of Simon Zukas in 1991 as a deputy minister in President Chiluba's government.

INTERRELIGIOUS CONFLICT AND DIALOGUE IN ZAMBIA

In keeping with its peaceful traditions, postcolonial Zambia is substantially inclined toward toleration of religious and cultural pluralism. This is not to say, however, that Zambians are inherently tolerant of other faiths, particularly those outside the Christian mainstream. President Kaunda clashed with the Jehovah's Witnesses (although this was admittedly more political than religious; they were prominent in Luapula but refused to vote, salute the flag, or sing the national anthem, provoking the wrath of the United National Independence Party (UNIP) and Kaunda and leading them to be stigmatized).[7] Other examples include blanket characterizations of African Muslims as Msene and the denunciation not of witchcraft per se (though this also occurs) but of individuals accused of witchcraft.

The fast-growing Pentacostalist Universal Church of the Kingdom of God, which originated in Brazil was shut down in December 2005 because former members alleged that it was engaging in Satanism and ritual murders. In fact, this was already the church's second act in Zambia; it had been banned earlier, in 1998, for similar reasons. Accusations of Satanism or witchcraft, regardless of their basis, are a tried and true method to squelch individuals and institutions seen as threatening or culturally unfamiliar. Indeed, Anderson Mazoka, a prominent politician and runner-up in the 2001 presidential race, was vilified in the late 1990s for his membership in the Freemasons, a group little understood in Zambia. His political opponents characterized the secret society as something approaching devil worship and sorcery. When these accusations quickly gained traction with the public, it put Mazoka on the defensive, eventually forcing him to renounce his membership in the organization. Similar cultlike qualities were attributed in the town of Livingstone in the 1990s to Indian Hindu shopkeepers who were the victims of mob justice after local residents accused them of ritual murders of several young Zambian children.

These incidents, and scattered other cases of intolerance notwithstanding, religiously driven violence in Zambia is, nonetheless, a rarity. In part, this can be attributed to the country's limited religious diversity wherein non-Christians represent but a tiny fraction of the populace. Cognizant of their status, minority groups tend to keep a low profile and avoid controversial political and social matters. Thus, as one of Africa's most solidly Christian states, Zambia has witnessed scant interreligious conflict. Moreover, the leaders of various Christian communities have demonstrated a capacity to work together for the common good of Zambia (such as the Oasis Forum) despite their doctrinal differences. This cooperative relationship may change, of course, as the evangelical brand of Christianity becomes increasingly influential and may come into conflict with the more established traditional Christian faiths, such as Roman Catholics and Anglicans. It is possible that mainline denominations will be threatened if they continue to lose their own congregations to the more stimulating evangelicals.

It is unlikely, however, that religion will form a significant line of political cleavage in Zambia in the future. Indeed, religion is just one of many sources of identity; ethnicity or tribe, language, class, party affiliation, and so on have been more consistent fault lines in society. Indeed, the failure of the 1996 Christian constitution to ignite durable tensions suggests that Zambia is not prepared to do battle over religious issues. Even politicians that would endeavor to stir up religious sentiments, for good or ill, are not likely to get far. It should be noted, for example, that Nevers Mumba, running on a largely religious platform, lost convincingly in 2001, whereas the privately religious Levy Mwanawasa won.

At bottom, religion is an important aspect of Zambian life. Since the late nineteenth century, religiosity has been expressed primarily through Christian faiths, but the spirituality of traditional beliefs—and some of the practices—remains embedded in Zambia's various cultures. At the same time, life in the early twenty-first century continues to be complex and increasingly difficult for the majority of Zambians. Indeed, challenges abound: Recurrent droughts and food shortages have already characterized the young decade, and AIDS, economic dislocation, rampant unemployment, and poverty continue to frustrate the aspirations of the majority of Zambians. Many take solace in their religious traditions. Thus, despite these myriad problems, Zambians' spirituality, which is personally held, and the strength of the churches as institutions contribute to a predominant worldview that is, if not necessarily consistently optimistic, certainly resilient.

NOTES

1. This section is drawn from Roberts, *A History of Zambia,* especially 73–76.

2. Roberts, *A History of Zambia,* 76.

3. The work of Patrick Chabal and Jean Pascal Daloz is culpable here. See Chabal and Daloz, *Africa Works,* 63–76.

4. See Ciekawy and Geschiere "Confronting Witchcraft."

5. Roberts, *A History of Zambia,* 180.

6. Seshamani, "A Hindu View of the Declaration of Zambia as a Christian Nation."

7. Roberts, *A History of Zambia,* 250.

3

Literature and the Media

Like many African countries, Zambia has a fairly recent and somewhat narrow literary tradition. Zambia stands in stark contrast, therefore, to those few countries that have produced the giants of African literature, such as Kenya, Nigeria, and South Africa, whose authors have received both African and global acclaim. Moreover, although the range of broadcast media available in Zambia has expanded widely in recent years as a result of technological improvements, print media are also limited in scope and number in Zambia. The limited reach of these written forms of communication stems from multiple factors, including the colonial legacy, the ethnolinguistic diversity and traditions of the Zambian population, and persistent economic problems.

Although the English language was introduced alongside British colonialism beginning in the 1890s, it was not until several decades later that indigenous languages were even made literate, when the languages were transcribed using the Latin alphabet, often to translate the Bible. Colonial-era schools, in which European missionary organizations were also predominant, also had a limited reach for many years, thus few Zambians had access to formal training in English, and even fewer had opportunities to gain literacy in their native tongues. In addition, numbering only about 11 million, Zambia's current population is relatively small for a country roughly the size of California. Although perhaps 50 percent of this population is urban—that is, concentrated in the larger urban areas such as those in the Copperbelt and Lusaka—the remainder is widely dispersed across a large territory. Rural populations tend to be vastly underserved in terms of resources, such as those for education, and access to media.

Whereas most Zambians, particularly in the rural areas, speak their birth tongue at home, English is the language of instruction in schools throughout the country, beginning in grade one in urban polyglot environments. At the latest, English education begins in grade three in rural primary schools, where virtually all of the students speak the same mother tongue. Some 80 percent of Zambians older than age 15 are literate in English, which is quite surprising given the country's history and its ethnolinguistic diversity. Yet, as these statistics reveal, not all Zambians become literate, or even fluent, in English, despite its place as the national language. Paradoxically, because of the nature of society, pedagogy, and the social trends discussed later, far fewer Zambians are fully literate in their native languages. Those who are typically receive instruction at higher education institutions, such as via the linguistics programs at the University of Zambia, for example; primary or secondary schools offer local first languages as a single course of study. Not surprisingly, therefore, only a small volume of works are published in local tongues.

Conversely, it is economic constraints, more so than illiteracy, that account for the relative paucity of writings in English. Zambia's publishing industry remains quite small, owing to a small domestic market. Of course, by far the most-read medium is the newspaper, and several are published in Zambia, albeit with relatively small, mostly urban-centered circulations. Because of costs of production and transport, it is not worthwhile for print media companies to supply Zambia's hinterlands; because of rural poverty, newspapers are a luxury item that few can afford with any regularity.

Given the paucity of books (whether produced domestically or internationally), and with access magazines and even newspapers limited, most Zambians rely upon the broadcast media for news and information as well as entertainment. Television signals are restricted mainly to the urban areas, and televisions are prohibitively expensive, hence radio is the principal means of conveying information throughout the country, although even radio signals are not accessible in all regions.

Two other means of communication—one very old, the oral tradition, and the other, quite new, the Internet—also merit discussion. The former is part of every Zambian community, embodied in centuries-old traditions, and the latter has only a limited reach. Nevertheless, both are important means of sustaining communities, customs, and, to some extent, language. Proceeding, therefore, from ancient to modern methods of disseminating information, culture, and entertainment, this chapter first examines the role of storytelling in Zambian culture and society, before turning to conventional approaches to literature and the media (both print and broadcast), and finally to the promise of comparatively new technologies like the Internet.

The Oral Tradition

Because Zambian ethnic groups have been literate for only about a century, historically, all groups relied on oral histories, including the telling of creation myths, proverbs, and folktales passed down through the generations. Although this tradition has been joined by the written word, the addition of writing serves as a complement to the oral histories rather than supplanting them. Indeed, even today villages have storytellers. Unlike in certain West African cultures, where this role is designated intergenerationally (and usually limited to males), in Zambian villages storytellers are simply men or women who have the ability to tell a good story and captivate an audience.

Storytelling is not limited to rural environments, of course, although modern forms of media and entertainment in urban areas—a phenomenon discussed later—indeed threatens to weaken the role of more traditional forms of transmitting culture and traditions from one generation to the next. Stories are generally told at home in the evening following the meal. In fact, an expression among the Bemba says, "If you tell a story during the day, your father will change into a monkey, your mother into a cold lump of porridge."[1] This prohibition on daytime stories, though not a hard and fast rule, is something most Bemba people have heard since childhood. Nonetheless, the stories tend to be interactive and performance-based, rather than simply the bedtime tale with which most readers are undoubtedly familiar. Thus, the stories tend to serve as both entertainment and, importantly, as a means of transmitting norms, values, and traditions important to and about the various cultures. They often deal with supernatural phenomena and contain not-so-subtle morality tales. Hence, even stories ostensibly for children have a rough edge to them. Like the well-known fairy tales of Hans Christian Anderson or the Brothers Grimm, Zambian folktales can be dark and occasionally violent.[2]

Virtually all of Zambia's ethnic groups have their own stories that have been passed on through the generations. The Tonga of Southern Province, for example, have stories that frequently center on their cattle ownership and traditions. Many groups, including the Tonga, employ animals as the main characters in their stories. Certain characteristics are associated with various animal species, and the strongest animals are often outwitted by more resourceful underdogs. In the "Tale of the Hare and the Elephant," for example, the hare is depicted as clever and cunning, notwithstanding his diminutive size. Those familiar with Zambian tales point out that animal characters have both familiar habits and forms to which audiences can relate, but they also permit the storyteller—and his audience—to use great imagination.[3]

The storytelling village tradition has been supplemented, and in some respects supplanted, by broadcast media, particularly radio, which has the capacity to reach far-flung areas of the country. Zambian radio has from time to time accommodated these traditions. For example, among the most popular programs in the 1970s and 1980s was *Phochedza M'Madzulo* (meaning "to hang around in the evening"). This weekly half-hour series of stories was broadcast in Nyanja and enjoyed great popularity, even in cosmopolitan Lusaka. A similar program, *Ifyabukaya* (meaning "things that you know"), offered stories in the Bemba language. Interestingly, *Ifyabukaya* has been recently revived and is once again on the air to be enjoyed by a new generation of Zambians.

The larger language groups, including Bemba, Nyanja, and Tonga, are widely spoken and not themselves endangered. Nevertheless, not surprisingly, many of the oral traditions of these, and certainly smaller groups, are today under threat, as people all over Zambia increasingly use English as a means of communication. Although folktales and other means of communication retain a certain intrinsic value even in English, their translation risks stripping them of much of their meaning. Of greater concern, this comes within a rapidly changing cultural milieu in which languages and traditions are being diluted or lost altogether at an increasing rate. Although many individual families maintain these traditions, of course, there is no equivalent in Zambia to the Griots of Senegal and Gambia, whose ancient role as keepers of oral tradition has preserved family and community stories for centuries. Each Griot passes the stories down to the next generation, and thus the stories are preserved for posterity. Lacking such an institution, Zambians are in danger of losing both family histories as well as important collective memories.

What was once oral has not, for the most part, been transformed into the written medium, however. As noted later in the chapter, the preservation of various cultural histories and folktales in literature—whether in a Zambian tongue or in English—has simply not occurred on an appreciable level. A few stories have made it to mass printings, but, by and large, the African oral tradition mostly has been captured through the work of scholars of ethnic history, many of them Western academicians.

The Establishment of a Literary Tradition

Roman Catholic priests, primarily from France, known as the White Fathers arrived in Zambia around 1891. Although their objectives were clearly distinct from those of the British South Africa Company officials who defined the modern dimensions of the territory, the Western religious communities were nonetheless part of the colonial enterprise. The White Fathers were active in what is now Northern Province, initially among the Mambwe and later the Bemba. After establishing several missions in the region, the White Fathers chose Bemba as one of the first languages for the literary translation of religious and educational materials. Among the earliest written texts included the first Bemba grammar in 1907 and a translation of the New Testament in 1923.[4] Prior to that time, many Africans of course had learned English in the first three decades of colonial rule, both in its spoken and written forms; however, there was no written-form African language. Eventually, both the spoken and written forms of iciBemba spread to other areas, particularly the Copperbelt and Luapula Provinces, where it became a lingua franca, initially among mine workers.

Based primarily in Northern Province, the White Fathers had to rely on educated Africans to help promulgate the new written language as well as promote literacy in English. Early on, this was done through missionary schools and the churches, rather than the state per se, during the colonial era. White clergy and laypeople relied heavily, therefore, on African lay preachers and teachers to disseminate the written language. Following independence in 1964, however, the teaching of written and spoken forms of Zambian languages was largely assumed by the country's primary and secondary schools.

For example, "in the Northern, Luapula, and Copperbelt Provinces, Bemba is the primary medium of instruction in grades 4–12.... Other efforts related to preserving and promoting the language include the regular publication of religious texts, the periodic publication of novels, poetry and cultural commentary, and the occasional audio recording of traditional songs." Although such efforts are laudatory, they have a direct and detrimental impact on Zambia's smaller ethnolinguistic groups. Indeed, whereas primary schools in Mongu, the regional capital of Western Province, will offer Lozi, like those in Kasama will offer Bemba, only 7 of the country's 73 languages are sanctioned for use in education. Thus, in addition to Lozi and Bemba and, of course, English, only Kaonde, Luvale, Lunda, Nyanja, and Tonga are privileged for use in education, mass media, and government documents.[5]

Popular Literature in English

Given the conditions described previously, Zambian authors face many challenges in their efforts to reach domestic audiences. Perhaps not surprisingly, then, they are not particularly well known internationally, either. One exception is Binwell Sinyangwe, author of two recent works in English, *Quills of Desire* (1996) and *A Cowrie of Hope* (2000). The first was published first by Baobab Books, once a thriving publisher in Harare, Zimbabwe, and later by Heinemann South Africa. Significantly, however, the latter book is the only book published in Heinemann's renowned African Writers Series by a Zambian author. Although this provides some indication of the international achievement of Sinyangwe, it is also emblematic of both the paucity of Zambian writers and (more distressingly) the difficulty of their accessing international publishing houses, a point that has been acknowledged by Sinyangwe himself.

Certainly, one of the factors behind Sinyangwe's success with *Cowrie of Hope* is the book's timely subject matter: a young widow struggling with a teenage daughter, the pervasiveness of poverty in the 1990s, corruption, and the ferocity of the AIDS epidemic. Indeed, *Cowrie of Hope* captures the desperation faced by many Zambians in the tumultuous 1990s, a decade that began with great democratic promise but ended with Zambians poorer and without a safety net, sicker from the ravages of AIDS and a crumbling health care system, and mourning democracy's decline. Women were impacted most severely. As Sinyangwe notes:

> The nineties were difficult years. They were the years of money first or else no friendship. And they were the years when the new disease of the world, the advent of the eighties, decided to sit down on a stool by the riverside and fish people like *cisense*.... They were not years to scratch your head or yield to the next flesh you ran into. They were dangerous years. Hard and poisonous.[6]

It is not that other Zambians are not writing, however, and a few are finding avenues to publish their work, including self-publication. For example, *Negotiating Blood* (year) is written by Hannilie H. Zulu, a Zambian woman. Zulu is the author of several books, including *The Little Bad Guy* (year). Books by Zambia's academic authors tend to find an outlet, too. Yet the local publishing industry is quite small (unlike, say, Zimbabwe or South Africa), which is also a limiting factor.

Literature in Indigenous Languages: Decline or Revival?

Some African countries have seen a surge in writing in indigenous languages, even by prominent authors. Although their books and stories necessarily reach a smaller audience than they would if produced initially in a European language, these authors are interested in promoting and preserving the culture and the language itself; indeed, studies show that some 50 percent of the world's languages, including half of Africa's estimated 800 languages, will disappear in this century. A conference sponsored by the United Nations Environment Programme (UNEP) in Kenya noted that 234 of the world's languages have already disappeared and that the Chikunda and Dema tongues, spoken in Zambia as well as Mozambique and Zimbabwe, are also in danger of extinction.

Partly in response to the threat to indigenous languages, some African writers, such as the renowned Kenyan author Ngugi wa Thiong'o, have opted to write only in their mother tongue (in Ngugi's case, Kikuyu). Most African writers, however, do not have that luxury. Because Ngugi was already an acclaimed author when he opted to write solely in Kikuyu, he was assured that his work would be translated, by others, into English, thus continuing to reach a broad Kenyan and worldwide readership. In recent years, African writers in other countries, including South Africa and Zimbabwe, have opted to write in an indigenous language. No such examples of this in Zambia are available internationally, and only a handful, mainly for educational purposes, are available in Zambia itself.

In any of the handful of bookstores one finds in the capital city, Lusaka, for example, few contain works by Zambian authors, with the exception of a smattering of local biographies, as well as study books and workbooks used in primary education. Indeed, educational publishing may offer relatively more outlets. The sector was represented by some 10 companies as of 2000; between 1966 and 1991, however, educational publishing was controlled by the state-owned Zambia Educational Publishing House. As noted, the local private publishing industry is small; moreover, few consumers have the resources to buy books, creating both a problem of demand and of supply.

MEDIA

Like many African countries, the state is the largest player in the media business. State-owned media is a legacy of the one-party state, in which the government was the only entity to disseminate information to the populace via print, television, and radio news, and it even controlled the broadcast of music and entertainment. The demise of the one-party state and the liberalization of politics in Zambia beginning in 1990, however, brought significant changes to the airwaves. Although the state still plays a major role and maintains its ownership of several key national media outlets, Zambia now has a small but vibrant privately owned media. The emergence first of private newspapers, followed by privately owned radio stations, has democratized access to information in Zambia. No longer are Zambians fed only the party line from government sources but are increasingly free to draw their own conclusions about social conditions, economics, ideology, and, especially, politics from a diverse array of outlets and viewpoints. Nonetheless, with their ability to draw on government subsidies, as well as upon advertising revenues, the state-owned media must be considered the dominant actors in the media marketplace even today.

Newspapers and Magazines

The Government-Owned Press

As noted, substantial government ownership of the press is not unique to Zambia, or even to Africa. Indeed, in much of Africa, the state ownership is itself a legacy of the colonial period, when European powers sought to control the dissemination of information and propaganda, principally to Europeans. With independence, African leaders merely assumed control of the state media apparatus and in some cases expanded it. Interestingly, however, Zambia's leading government-owned newspaper, *The Times of Zambia,* was privately held until 1975—11 years after independence. Zambia's two leading government-owned newspapers are *The Times* and *The Daily Mail.* Both papers, which are controlled by the state-owned media company, claim independence on their mastheads: *The Daily Mail,* for example, insists that it serves "the Nation without Fear or Favour." Yet on closer inspection, these assertions strain credulity.

After 1991, periodic pledges were made to privatize the government-owned press. After all, it had been a tool of the Kenneth Kaunda regime for much of its 27-year reign. Yet Kaunda's successor, Frederick Chiluba and the Movement for Multiparty Democracy (MMD), found that *The Times* and the *Daily,* as it is commonly called, could be as useful tools for their own propaganda purposes as they had been for their predecessors in the United National Independence Party (UNIP). Hence, the papers were never privatized and toed as progovernment a line under the nominally democratic government of Chiluba as they had under Kaunda. What this means is that the government had a ready and widely read outlet for any statement or position it wished to put in the public domain. In addition, the papers were effectively proscribed from engaging in any criticism of government policies or, certainly, the president. On the contrary, the editorials consistently praised presidential maneuvers that earned criticism elsewhere, and the reporting contained a progovernment slant. This pattern continues under President Levy Mwanawasa.

Although in many respects the Mwanawasa government is more politically liberal than its predecessor, and some strides have been made in regard to transparency and accountability under Mwanawasa's presidency since January 2002, the press remains subject to political influence and pressures. For obvious reasons, the editorial pages are loath to criticize and, in fact, heap considerable praise on the incumbent government (certainly the president, although occasionally out-of-step ministers or MPs are criticized). More troubling, however, are the largely tacit constraints placed on reporters. The impact of state ownership and political obeisance to the government in power is not simply limited to the editors; it also affects the kind of stories that are reported in the papers and the way in which they are presented. Thus, whereas decidedly nonpolitical stories—such as those reporting on social or cultural events or business news, for example—lack any perceptible bias, political stories are invariably slanted toward the ruling MMD party and especially President Mwanawasa.

The Private Press

Zambia has an active and often quite intrepid private press that provides at least a partial corrective to the favoritism of the state media. Prior to the political liberalization of the 1990s, efforts to develop private newspapers typically fell flat. One, *The Sunday Post,* was published for a few months in the 1980s before being forced to close. Today, clearly the most prominent of the private newspapers is *The Post* (unrelated to the earlier paper of similar name). *The Post* was launched as a weekly newspaper by several concerned businessmen and a number of talented journalists in July 1991, just as the Kaunda regime was instituting new political reforms. When *The Post* began, there was only one other privately owned paper, the limited-circulation *National Mirror.* Emerging on the scene commensurate with the MMD and the liberalization of Zambian politics, the then *Weekly Post* quickly became known as a sharp critic of the Kaunda government during its last days. In fact, *The Post* was a major voice of opposition politicians and members of civil society. Its mission statement and editorial policy, which can be found on *The Post*'s Web site, says in part: "Our political role is to question the policies and actions of the authorities and all those who wield or aspire to wield social, economic and political power over the lives of ordinary people. We shall aim to protect and promote the newly-emerging democratic political culture, in which the fundamental rights and freedoms of individuals are guaranteed, through campaigning on issues that arise from our own investigations, reporting and analysis."

Although *The Post* certainly aided the MMD in its rise to power in October 1991, the paper maintained a truly independent voice and did not hesitate to criticize actions by the Chiluba government. In fact, the criticism leveled at the MMD government by *The Post* generated incredulity and occasionally vicious counterattacks from the targets of that criticism and their political supporters. Editor in Chief Fred M'membe and several of his top lieutenants and journalists at *The Post* faced repeated harassment at the hands of politicians and security officials. Occasionally, *Post* officials faced violent threats. Although *Post* reporters and editors largely avoided physical harm, such as the torture meted out to Zimbabwean journalists beginning in the late 1990s, they were frequently targeted by state officials. As the MMD became increasingly authoritarian in the 1990s, the journalists, including M'membe, were arrested numerous times on specious charges. The first was in 1993, and other prominent instances occurred in 1996 and 1997, although the events were not limited to those three.

The international Committee to Protect Journalists observed in 1997 that *The Post* had been served with more than 100 writs by the MMD between 1991 and 1997, noting that "There are more court cases pending against journalists in Zambia than anywhere else in Africa, the state's intention being to financially incapacitate the independent press. While the overburdened judiciary has shown autonomy in the disposition of some of these cases, it has appeared influenced by the executive branch in others."[7] Yet Zambia no longer claims this dubious distinction. Moreover, in every case, *The Post* was vindicated in court, which was all the more impressive considering the Zambian judiciary has only partial political independence from the executive, particularly under the Kaunda and Chiluba regimes. Even more surprisingly, given the political environment at the time, in 1996 a coalition of Zambian journalists, donors, and others managed to secure certain constitutional reforms that actually served to limit the government's power to silence media critics. The changes eliminated the government's capacity to ban publications; however, the harassment of the free press continued nevertheless. These legal victories, however, actually burnished *The Post*'s profile in Zambia and globally, where it particularly attracted the attention of international media watchdogs, such as the Committee to Protect Journalists and the Center for Public Integrity. Certainly, *The Post* played an instrumental role in strengthening democracy and the voices of opposition in Zambia, both directly and indirectly by emboldening other critics of the government.

For the most part, the public remained loyal to *The Post,* as its sustained readership and popularity attest. Zambians, indeed, rely on *The Post* as "the paper that digs deeper," although some have occasionally criticized it over the years as engaging in tabloid-style attack journalism. On the whole, however, the paper's overall contribution to information sharing, democracy, and public opinion in Zambia far outweigh these criticisms. In the wake of *The Post*'s success, a large number of other private newspapers have emerged. These have varying levels of popularity, journalistic quality, and editorial integrity, but it is a testament to the liberalized media environment that, in Zambia's urban centers, at least, consumers have access to a wide range of media viewpoints.

At bottom, *The Post* has maintained its popularity, often against overwhelming odds. In the mid-1990s, it went to a daily format, which was a reflection of its growing prominence. Today, it has a daily circulation of about 20,000–25,000. By contrast, the *Times* and *Daily* have circulations of between

15,000 and 20,000 copies per day. Newspapers tend to reach urban areas only, and towns receive copies several days late, if at all. The more remote regions of the country may never receive one of these putatively national newspapers. Even in the more populous areas, however, newspapers can be prohibitively expensive for many Zambians and must be considered elite items. The price of newsprint has increased some 500 percent since the 1990s, which, of course, has a direct impact on the cover price. On the positive side, all newspapers are read more widely than their first-run printings would suggest because it is common in Zambia for people to share copies of the paper once they have read them.

Radio and Television

Like newspaper ownership and distribution, the radio airwaves were also liberalized in the 1990s. National television broadcast rights remained solely with the government, although with the emergence of satellite television and, later, the Internet, a growing number of Zambians, particularly among the urban middle and upper classes, now have access to other forms of television news, music, and entertainment. Notwithstanding liberalization, however, the largest and most influential local broadcaster, both for television and radio, remains the government-owned Zambia National Broadcasting Company (ZNBC).

ZNBC occupies a sprawling broadcast facility in Lusaka's Longacres neighborhood. Indicating the importance of the national state-controlled media, this imposing complex is surrounded by a large metal fence and is guarded heavily to protect the facility from coup plotters real and imagined. (ZNBC was briefly occupied in 1997 by a drunken and disgruntled band of army soldiers who announced that they had effected a coup. Their control never got beyond the radio station, however, and they were promptly arrested.)

ZNBC offers three radio stations, which are heard throughout the country. Radio One broadcasts in the seven major languages spoken in each of Zambia's nine provinces, as described previously: Bemba, Kaonde, Lozi, Lunda, Luvale, Nyanja, and Tonga. Radio Two offers both English and vernacular programming, whereas Radio 4 offers only English-language fare. All the stations offer mixed formats of music, talk, and dramatic programs. As in most African countries, radio remains the principal source of national and international information for Zambians; there are an estimated 1.9 million radios in the country as of 2004. Although officially there are 19 AM and 5 FM stations (both public and private) to which those radios may be tuned, in reality, very few of these have the capacity to be heard outside of a very narrow listening range.

When compared with radio, television is a far more restricted medium that has at least three major limitations. The first relates to demographic factors. Zambia's overall poverty means that a television, which would consume more than a year's wages for many households, is simply beyond the reach of the vast majority of consumers. Perhaps it is surprising that, given these constraints, Zambians own as many televisions, an estimated half-million, as they do. Of course, another complication concerns the government's provision of rural infrastructure, which is such that many rural dwellers have little access to reliable electricity, if they have any at all. In addition, ZNBC lacks the capacity to broadcast to some of the far-flung reaches of Zambia's rather expansive geographic territory. Thus, whereas radio is widely available and batteries or solar-powered units may assist those Zambians with radios but without access to electricity, ZNBC-TV, for example, does not even have adequate signal strength to reach much of Zambia's Northwestern Province, including the large towns of Siavonga and Lundazi. Zambia has a reported nine broadcast television stations, including ZNBC and foreign signals. These numbers are a bit misleading, however, because some of these are so-called repeaters (the same broadcast on a different frequency). In most instances, Zambians without access to a satellite receiver can expect to tune in two stations, at best: ZNBC 1 and ZNBC 2.

A second major limitation of television in Zambia is that state-owned broadcasters are constrained by the type of programming they can offer. New programs are expensive to produce, hence Zambian fare consists principally of news broadcasts and the occasional talk show or interview program. Foreign shows are arguably more popular, but the cost of buying syndicated television programs from the United States, United Kingdom, or elsewhere is also high; thus, in terms of entertainment, Zambians are typically limited in their options to older or obscure television shows, such as reruns of the U.S. soap opera *The Bold and the Beautiful,* or films that in the United States were made for the so-called straight-to-video market. Religious programs from abroad are also common; for example, televangelists from the United States, Australia, and elsewhere (as well as from Zambia) are frequently seen, and not just on Sunday.

Finally, the government places political restrictions on television and radio producers. Even under the relatively liberal Mwanawasa government, reporters, editors, and producers face tacit and occasionally explicit pressures not to challenge the official party line. This was worse under Chiluba and worse still under the Kaunda regime. As recently as 1996, however, a popular television show host was fired for participating in and airing an interview with a presidential candidate from the opposition. It is, therefore, a difficult environment for independently minded journalists who are uncomfortable

incessantly toeing the party line. It is more problematic, of course, for Zambian television (and print and radio) viewers whose only source of television news is ZNBC. Nonetheless, most Zambians are keenly aware of the biases inherent in the state-owned media, and, therefore, most are inclined to discount the progovernment reporting as partisan.

A clear benefit of the media liberalization that has occurred, however haltingly, since 1991, and which accelerated after the 2001 election of Levy Mwanawasa, has been the proliferation of news and entertainment sources, which present options to consumers beyond ZNBC. Previously, the roles of *The Post* newspaper and others in the print media were described. *The Post,* with its intrepid and occasionally brazen editors, was in many respects a trailblazer for other nongovernment sources. Consumers now have a choice, particularly in radio listening options, although, admittedly, most broadcasters adhere to apolitical programming formats.

Among private broadcasters, perhaps the most successful to date has been Radio Phoenix, one of the first nongovernment stations on the air. Founded by local entrepreneur Errol Hickey in 1994, Radio Phoenix offers a variety of programming: music, news, talk, and discussion. With its first music DJs adopting monikers like "Bad Mamma Jamma" and "Amazing Grace," Radio Phoenix managed to carve out a niche for itself. It achieved a contemporary, Western feel in a country that had previously had only limited radio options. Like its state-owned counterparts, Radio Phoenix also features call-in programs, which themselves have been significantly aided by the proliferation of cell phones beginning in the late 1990s. More importantly, the competition provided by Radio Phoenix and, later, other private broadcasters actually improved ZNBC's offerings.

A number of other private broadcasters have also emerged, including Breeze FM Radio, Q FM, and Radio Choice. In addition, the churches have joined in the airwaves with religious-based programming options. Yasane Radio is sponsored by the Catholic Church in Zambia. Radio Christian Voice, which was described in chapter 2, offers syndicated programs originating from the organization Christian Voice, based in the United Kingdom. A station called Icengelo broadcasts principally in the city of Ndola, in Zambia's Copperbelt Province, and offers Roman Catholic–themed programming in the Bemba language.

Whereas private media have more flexibility and autonomy to produce and air the kind of programming they see fit, like their print media counterparts, they are not immune to political interference and harassment. Indeed, at the height of the 2001 election campaign, Radio Phoenix ran afoul of the government and was effectively taken off the air for several weeks. Its *Let the People Talk* call-in program resulted in criticism of then-president Chiluba and the

MMD, which responded by suspending Radio Phoenix during the height of the campaign. (It is important to note that the government did not use an overtly political rationale but argued instead that the station's license had lapsed and this was grounds for its temporary closure.)

Needless to say, the government's intimidation sent a chill through private media circles, as well as the wider populace, that censorship of opposition views was still in full force in Zambia. The Radio Phoenix experience was doubly ironic because Hickey was well connected with a number of key senior MMD figures and was on speaking terms with President Chiluba himself. In any event, like the phoenix of lore, Radio Phoenix was soon back on the air, although chastened, as were many of the private media outlets in Zambia. The experiences of Radio Phoenix, *The Post,* and other independents, especially under Chiluba's regime from 1991 to 2001, drove home the parlous nature of independent media in Zambia. Yet they also had the effect of making people treasure these sources of information, opinion, and entertainment all the more. Private broadcasters thus play an increasingly vital role in supporting the expansion and strengthening of Zambia's nascent democracy.

Satellite Television: Democratizing the Airwaves or Cultural Imperialism?

As discussed previously, foreign, that is non-Zambian, programs have been a fixture on the state-owned ZNBC almost since independence. Quintessentially U.S. shows, from *The Jeffersons* to *Star Trek* to *The Love Boat* to soaps and miniseries, as well as British dramas and comedies were routinely shown on Zambian television in the 1970s and 1980s, especially. It was more a reflection of the increased expense of offering these programs than of the maturation and expansion of ZNBC's local programming capacity that led to a reduction of foreign offerings in recent years. Nonetheless, those Zambian families that could afford televisions clearly have long been exposed to foreign ideas and imagery. Although this led inevitably to some degree of exaltation of the foreign—which was seen as exotic, desirable, and worthy of imitation and gave rise to an extremely stylized view of life in the United States and Britain—ZNBC, at least, always maintained a small stable of local shows and news broadcasts that kept the network essentially Zambian.

The proliferation of satellite dishes since the early 1990s has begun to alter this essential Zambian quality in subtle, if disturbing, ways. To be sure, satellite dishes are available to only a tiny elite. Moreover, access to CNN, BBC, MTV, and South Africa's M-NET arguably offers nothing more than greater information about the world, a wider range of opinion, and more diverse entertainment. Yet at the same time, many of these elites—the children of politicians, businesspeople, diplomats, and so forth, who enjoy access to education, travel, and other opportunities—are some of the people who will eventually inherit the levers of power in Zambia. Their worldview is therefore important (see chapter 2). To the extent that they are inclined to exalt the foreign (particularly Western) and not completely understand (and in some cases denigrate) the Zambian bodes poorly for the preservation of Zambian culture, ideas, language, and traditions over the long term.

It is important not to overstate the role of satellite television in this phenomenon, which some refer to as the dilution of Zambian culture. As noted, satellite television, for example, reaches a fairly limited audience. Clearly, there are other sources of what critics label Western cultural imperialism that showcase (and directly and indirectly promote) Western norms and values, many of which are addressed in this book, including music, dance, movies (mostly on video or CD), food, and the proliferation of English at the expense of indigenous languages. Moreover, it is important to point out the democratizing aspects of various media options and opportunities. Quite simply, more sources means less (state) control and more options for more people. In addition, access to information can aid the awareness and diffusion of international norms, such as those pertaining to human rights, women's rights, and so forth. Nevertheless, the diminution of Zambian content remains a cause for concern. Virtually all satellite imagery comes today from Zambia's far more developed neighbor, South Africa. In addition to beaming in U.S. programming on these channels, as noted previously, and, increasingly, Nigerian programs as well, South African music, dance, pop culture, and—not to be underestimated— South Africa products are also heavily promoted. Zambian news and information are sometimes not even available through the satellite linkages; therefore, elites are often faced with a choice: Zambian or South African. The proliferation and popularity of South African retail outlets in Zambia speak to the choice many Zambians are increasingly making. This affects more than simply consumer habits, however; the bombardment of Zambians with South African and Western imagery inevitably impacts the way in which people conceive of their culture and society in relation to others.

The World Wide Web and Zambian Connectivity

Access to information was often controlled by single-party governments in postcolonial Africa, and, as noted earlier, Zambia was no exception. Following independence, the Kaunda-led state acquired the broadcast media and by 1975 had established state control over the print media as well. Dissent was both implicitly and explicitly discouraged. Communication was similarly limited: Telephones were extremely rare and service was expensive and limited to the urban areas, and the legacy of this continues today with fewer than 90,000 landline telephones in the country. Consequently, the dissemination of information from one part of Zambia to another was dependent on the state and the particular prism it offered. Oral traditions alleviated this somewhat, but even then the geographic scope of modern Zambia was simply incompatible with this form of communication over a very large swath of its territory. The liberalization of media ownership in the 1990s certainly led to greater access to more diverse sources of information for more Zambians. Nonetheless, as observed, newspapers are both expensive to produce and to purchase, and the readership of small newspapers remains quite limited to a narrow elite. Television and even radio stations suffer similar constraints, thus the number of private actors and the breadth of viewpoints is still outnumbered by their state-run counterparts.

Increasingly, cell phones and the Internet have acted as an additional means of democratizing access to information in Zambia, as they have elsewhere in Africa. The rapid increase in cellular phone availability and affordability has meant that their use has become widespread. As of 2003, an estimated 241,000 cell phones were in use in Zambia, and this figure undoubtedly will continue to rise. Nonetheless, at a price of around $50 each, exclusive of the cost of calls, cell phones still remain out of reach for the vast majority of Zambians. It is not uncommon, however, for families to share phones to economize. In addition, the Internet is rapidly expanding in Zambia. The Internet emerged out of the University of Zambia (UNZA), which developed a pilot e-mail program (UNZANET) between 1991 and 1994. In 1994, Zambia became only the second sub-Saharan country, after South Africa, to establish an international Internet connection. That same year, the Internet service provider Zamnet was established to sell Internet service, although Zamnet did not begin operating until 1995 through a land connection in Cape Town, South Africa. Zamnet subsequently developed direct satellite links with the United States and the United Kingdom in 1997 and 1999, respectively.

Internet access is now common in most large business environments, certainly those with international linkages, and Internet cafes are increasingly common in even Zambia's midsize cities. It remains expensive, however, in part because of the substantial dependence on dial-up/landlines, although the proliferation of wireless technologies will surely bring these costs down in the future (as has occurred in the case of cellular phones). For the time being, however, Internet access in the home is limited to the most elite Zambian families. In 2003, Zambia ranked among the lowest number of subscribers in southern Africa, with just more than 68,000 Internet users, despite its position as one of the longest users of the Internet. Nonetheless, these figures should be taken with a grain of salt because Internet accounts, like newspapers, phones, and radios, tend to be shared between many individuals; the actual number of users is undoubtedly much higher.

It is important not to overstate the current or potential impact of cellular and computer technologies in Zambia in the near term; it remains a severely impoverished country. Where nearly 80 percent of the populace lives on less than $1 a day, the purchase of a mobile phone or even connecting to the Internet remains out of reach. As discussed, similar constraints hold for the purchase of a newspaper, a television, or a novel. Nonetheless, information has become less state-controlled and more democratic since 1991 and still more so since 2001. By sharing resources, Zambians now have the opportunity, at least, to gain a much more complete and accurate picture about issues that affect their world, their country, and their lives than at any time in the past.

NOTES

1. The White Fathers' "Bemba-English Dictionary" *lushimi,* quoted in Lehmann, *Folktales from Zambia,* 16.

2. Saha, *History of the Tonga Chiefs,* 95.

3. Ibid., 95–96.

4. Spitulnik and Kashoki, "Bemba: A Brief Linguistic Profile."

5. Ibid.

6. Sinyangwe, *A Cowrie of Hope,* 30.

7. "Zambia." Committee to Protect Journalists.

4

Art, Architecture, and Housing

Art

The traditional artwork of central and western Africa—such as the ceramic sculptures of the Nok culture in northern Nigeria dating from 500 B.C., the elaborate fifteenth-century carvings from the Kongo Kingdom, Makonde masks of Mozambique, the royal kente cloth of the Ashanti people of Ghana—and even more contemporary forms—such as Shona sculpture from Zimbabwe, a tradition that dates only from the mid-twentieth century—are highly prized among Western galleries and private collectors. By contrast, Zambia has few internationally renowned artists or styles, although the peoples of Zambia have a long tradition of arts and craft work, including sculpture, beadwork, and basketry. A number of expatriate graphic artists and painters also have made a home in Zambia and have made a noteworthy contribution to art and culture in Zambia.

Painting actually has its origins in ancient rock paintings, done on the walls of caves, and a number of sites remain around Zambia. These include Nachikufu Cave in Mpika as well as the Mkomo Rock Shelter in Eastern Province, near Chipata, which contains rock paintings that date from the Iron Age. Among the oldest known examples are found at Nsalu Cave, near Kanona, which was excavated in the 1940s and contains cave drawings done by hunter-gatherers perhaps 3,000 years ago. These Stone Age rock drawings and paintings are found widely in southern Africa, including in Zimbabwe, Botswana, and South Africa, and provide rare and important clues about the lives and habits of prehistoric peoples in the region.

Flash forward several millennia and it is apparent that only a negligible tradition of painting continues in modern Zambia. In fact, contemporary painting has largely been the preserve of expatriates or Westerners who settled in Zambia. A number of them, such as Cynthia Zukas, have earned some recognition both within and outside Zambia for their work on wildlife painting, abstracts, as well as in other media, such as wood and ceramics. The highly regarded Bente Lorenz is in this latter category, and her studio in Lusaka's Longacres neighborhood has long served as an exhibition site as well as a training ground for young artists. Perhaps the most famous indigenous painter was Henry Tayali, who died at age 43 in 1987 but whose legacy lives on in the eponymous gallery, the Tayali Visual Arts Centre, located in Lusaka's Showgrounds. Tayali worked mostly in oils and woodblock prints and specialized in abstract and semiabstract painting. Tayali was supportive of young artists and the culture of painting in the country, including through his appointed role as artist at the University of Zambia, which he took up in 1976. Although Zambia still has no schools of the fine arts, materials are expensive, and funding is limited, the Tayali Centre and other galleries and facilities around Zambia nevertheless play vital roles by exhibiting the work of young artists.

Another avenue taken by a few Zambian artists to promote and exhibit their work is online studios, either through their own Web sites or established art sites on the Internet. For those who are able to access the technology, such avenues can give Zambian artists a truly global audience. In addition, the Zambia National Visual Arts Council, established in 1989, works to promote awareness of the arts and the interests of both new and established artists in Zambia. The recent book *Art in Zambia,* under the byline of local artist Gabriel Ellison and the Zambia National Visual Arts Council, is one such important effort.[1]

Functional Art and Handicrafts

In the precolonial period, the vast majority of artwork in Zambia was not simply for esthetic value but served a functional purpose. Basketry certainly falls in this category, as does furniture, cookware, and so on, much of which is now considered artwork, regarded as collectibles, and sold internationally. Interestingly, whereas colonialism had a salutary impact on the proliferation of graphic arts in Zambia (indeed, most of the first generation of Zambian painters that emerged in the mid-twentieth century were of European stock, as noted previously) and spurred interest in art for art's sake, colonialism also contributed to the decline of traditional art forms and the cultural ceremonies and specific functions that spawned them. Only in recent years have many of these arts seen something of a resurgence, in part because of the revival of some long-neglected cultural traditions (see chapter 7).

Masking

The practice of mask making, which is essentially limited to areas of North Western Province among the Chokwe and related groups and Eastern Province, is one such activity that has seen renewed interest. The Makishi masks of North Western Province, for example, depict standard characters that are now seen in public performances of traditional ceremonies. Crafted from a variety of materials, including animal hides, wood, feathers, and fibers such as sisal, traditional masks and mask making chiefly served religious, medicinal, or other ritual purposes rather than as art, per se. The Chokwe have three varieties of masks: sacred masks called *cikungu* are worn only by chiefs, circumcision masks, and dance masks. The chief's mask is in stylized human form, made of resin on a wooden frame. Initiation masks can represent people or animals such as the antelope; these are considered rare among collectors because they are supposed to be destroyed after the ceremonies. The dancers' masks represent either male or female ancestors, although all of the dancers are male. The Chokwe also carve a number of animal masks.[2]

Zambians from Eastern Province, particularly among the Chewa (who also reside in Malawi), are well known for their Nyau masks, which are worn only by initiated males. The Nyau masks are highly individualized depictions, which in the past were seen only within a highly secretive, fear-inspiring initiation and funeral rituals. "There are three types of masks among the Chewa. The first two, a feathered spirit mask and a wooden face mask, are used to represent spirits of the dead. The third, known collectively as *nyau yolemba,* are large zoomorphic basketwork structures, most of which represent wild animals, though cars, cattle, sorcerers, and Europeans are also represented."[3] Since the 1950s and 1960s, however, Nyau ceremonies have lost some of their more clandestine and terrifying attributes and are often performed for outsiders. (The Nyau ceremonies are described in chapter 8.)

Basket Making, Weaving, and Carving

Baskets are woven of bamboo, various grasses, sisal, or bark. They are typically put to a variety of practical uses, including as storage, for ceremonies, for carrying goods, as well as for decoration. Unlike other art forms, such as masking and carving, which are the exclusive province of men, both men and women participate in basket making. Although it is practiced throughout Zambia, the basketry of the Lozi and Mbunda, both of whom reside in

Western Province, is particularly renowned. Other groups, too, have traditions of weaving things like mats for sitting or eating or for tableware. The abundance of materials and relatively simplicity and sturdy construction mean that basketwork is fairly ubiquitous.

A similarly wide availability of limestone, wood, soapstone, and various clays facilitate carving and sculpting, and a small community of local sculptors has emerged, some of whom have earned international recognition. Of course, these media are not only the preserve of name artists. Indeed, clay sculpture is commonly used in ritual: for example, in initiation ceremonies for girls and as part of the marriage rites in the Bemba tradition. Clay figurines representing certain characters, and imbued with meaning, are crafted by women and displayed; the bride and, occasionally, the groom must commit these meanings to memory and identify them in the course of various initiations. It is unlikely that much of this contemporary work, which in any event is not intended for display, would find its way into the collection of any but the most avid aficionados of anthropological art.

A relatively thriving market in what professional artists and art connoisseurs derisively refer to as "airport art" consists of everything from drums carved from tree trunks, masks, and stools to human or animal figurines to soapstone chess boards and the like. These curios, aimed largely but not entirely at the tourist market, of course are found for sale not only in airports (although there they routinely fetch the highest prices) but also in various locations in and around Lusaka and other cities. They are typically displayed for sale along the side of a well-traveled roadway, outside the entrance to major tourist sites, such as Victoria Falls in Livingstone, or in a designated marketplace, such as in the Kabwata neighborhood in Lusaka, rather than in a retail establishment or a studio. In fact, similar curios are found in virtually all sub-Saharan African countries that have even a modicum of tourist traffic. As in most African countries, the prices of these goods in Zambia are almost invariably subject to bargaining, whether the purchaser is a foreigner or Zambian.

To the trained eye, this so-called airport art has limited artistic value, at best; the work has a certain uniformity—one carved rhinoceros is virtually indistinguishable from the next—resulting in presentation and representation that resembles mass production. Yet each of these pieces is hand carved and polished and has some measure of artistry to it. Reproducing a richly detailed, perfectly proportioned bust of a human head by hand, for example, is hardly an easy undertaking and requires more than a modicum of skill. Moreover, although not destined for Western or Zambian galleries, this curio art serves an important niche, both for souvenirs from Zambia as well as for relatively inexpensive home decorations for many contemporary Zambian households, ironically seeking an African decor for their otherwise Western domiciles. Moreover, the sales of the various sculptures and other items provide the petit artisans, generally men, who create them with a vital source of income and livelihood. (Men are responsible for woodwork and carving, whereas women typically work with ceramic materials, including throwing pots and firing kilns.) Notwithstanding their economic and even artistic merits, however, it is more than a little problematic that many, if not most, carvings are made of wood. The demand for these items contributes to an already massive deforestation problem not only in Zambia but also in the region as a whole. Over the long term, ecological pressures may actually threaten the very livelihoods of the artists and artisans that depend on natural materials.

ARCHITECTURE AND HOUSING

Traditional Forms of Architecture

In Zambia's larger cities, including Lusaka and Ndola, the familiar glass, steel, brick, and concrete construction of Western-style buildings is everywhere apparent. For the most part, although many (but not all) structures are adapted for a semitropical climate, whether for residential, commercial, or industrial use, there is little that is uniquely Zambian, or even African, about them. Even in small municipalities, such as Chongwe in Central Province or Serenje in Northern Province, such forms predominate in town or administrative centers, which, at the very least, are marked by their drab government office building and a central store. Commercial forms range from the trademark high rises of Lusaka's skyline to the low one- and two-story Edwardian buildings that have characterized the architecture of Livingstone since the colonial era. In the main, urban-area housing is similarly varied, although also within the confines of Western and Western-inspired styles. House types range from colonial-style villas (some built in that era, others recently) to multiunit apartment complexes to the ubiquitous small, unadorned brick or cinder-block structures typically found in the poorer urban neighborhoods as well as the high-density residential areas, also known as compounds.

Barely on the outskirts of any town or city, however, and certainly in more rural and remote areas of the country, one encounters a distinctly different style of architecture, including buildings whose essential design has remained unchanged for centuries. Throughout Zambia, traditional buildings were typically constructed of bamboo and mud or pole and mud construction and had thatch roofs made of elephant grass or *mupani* grass; this ancient method is still in use today throughout Zambia. In the latter

Several high-rise office buildings punctuate Lusaka's downtown skyline. Courtesy of the author.

part of the nineteenth century, missionaries introduced brick making, and this method remains commonly used in home construction throughout the country, although in remote rural areas one is less likely to find many structures composed of brick.

The basic styles of traditional homes varied only slightly, and most were regarded as short-term abodes. Among the Bemba, for example, a cluster of huts, constituting a village of sorts, would be placed near hunting grounds and places in which land had been cleared for cultivation; after several years, when these fields were exhausted, the community would move to a new area. The Tonga traditionally raised cattle in the precolonial era, as they do today. Although the Tonga began to concentrate subsequently more on farming, their earlier lifestyle also favored transient living conditions, accentuated by their politically decentralized structure. Even the Lozis, claimants of a strong, centralized kingdom that predated colonialism, had seasonal migrations that corresponded with the annual expansion of the Zambezi River floodplain, which made parts of the kingdom uninhabitable for months. In short, throughout Zambia, traditional housing was seldom built to last more than a few years, and in some cases far fewer than that.

The arrival of Europeans, first as missionaries and traders and subsequently as settlers, had a profound impact on architecture, as it did on virtually all other aspects of traditional Zambian life. They brought with them European styles and building techniques, such as the far more durable brickwork construction noted previously. Initially, however, much of it, too, had an impermanent quality. By and large, rural housing and residential existence remained the same for many years, particularly in the remote parts of the colony. Importantly, however, in urban and periurban areas (those surrounding cities and towns), the kinds of housing made available to whites and, later, Asians—and the areas in which they were permitted to reside—were of far superior quality to that available to blacks.

Colonial Influences

Homes built in the colonial period varied widely. For many Africans, colonialism meant the emergence of mass housing in large urban compounds, such as those that emerged in Lusaka and around the copper mines in Ndola and Kitwe. Africans migrated to the mines and the cities in search of wage work, as colonial authorities introduced hut taxes and a cash economy. Many of the whites who initially came to Zambia worked as managers and mine bosses. Because their residency was always regarded as of limited duration, their early houses were spartan and impermanent, reflecting the transient nature of their employment on the mines. These structures were hot, inadequate, and ill-suited to the climate, usually constructed with tin roofs imported from South Africa over a wood frame. As the period of company rule under the British South Africa Company came to an end in the 1920s and Northern Rhodesia became a largely self-governing crown colony, greater numbers of white settlers arrived, becoming farmers and traders, as well as an Indian merchant class. As more Europeans began to settle in Northern Rhodesia, particularly after the turn of the century, however, houses became sturdier, more elaborate, and better adapted to the Zambian environment. These usually included a single-story main house with a veranda plus servants' quarters. Following independence in 1964, when many whites left the new Zambia, these homes were purchased by African elites. Recent construction tends to correspond to this style: brick or cement cinder-block construction, plastered over and painted, typically white, with a broad veranda and a single story, which contributes to keeping the homes cool in the seasonally hot Zambian climate (even today, air conditioning is not widely found in most homes, including those owned by elites, and central heat is unheard of, despite June and July temperatures as low as the mid-40s in some regions). Given Zambia's voracious termites and wood-boring ants, buildings constructed of or clad in wood are virtually nonexistent, although fancier structures will have wooden parquet flooring inside as well as wooden doors and trim. Roofs are generally kiln-dried ceramic tile or corrugated tin.

Shiwa Ng'andu

One example of a colonial-era home in Zambia deserves special mention, not because it is typical in the country but because it is so extraordinary. The opulent, even excessive estate built at Shiwa Ng'andu by Sir Stewart Gore-Browne was begun in 1920 and completed nearly a decade later. Sir Stewart, a former colonel in the British Army, became something of a legend in Zambian history. In the years of colonial rule when blacks were not allowed to participate in their own governance, Gore-Browne was the member for African interests in the Northern Rhodesia Legislative Assembly from 1939 to 1951. He was a staunch advocate for African political rights, a leading supporter of Kenneth Kaunda in the 1950s and 1960s, and a member of the United National Independence Party (UNIP) until his death in 1967 at the age of 84. Yet it was Sir Stewart's estate at Shiwa Ng'andu that outlives even the memory of its builder.

The enormous 23,000-acre Shiwa Ng'andu estate lies some 65 kilometers (40 miles) from Mpika in Northern Province. At the heart of the estate lies Shiwa House, which can only be described as "Part Tuscan manor house, part grand English ancestral home, and all completely unexpected and out of place in this remote corner of the African bush. Surely, only a madman or a megalomaniac could have built such a place."[4] As one chronicler describes, "More than anywhere I had ever seen, Shiwa Ngandu seemed to symbolize the arrogance, paternalism, vision, and sheer bloody-mindedness of British colonials in Africa."[5] In short, Shiwa House was a tangle of contradictions, just like its master.

Gore-Browne, who had established his first house at Shiwa by 1914, spent the next several years designing the great house himself, inspired by various European architectural influences. The final product contained at least 40 rooms, including a library, dining room, an inner courtyard, and indoor plumbing. The house was filled with statues, paintings of Gore-Browne forebears and other noteworthy Britons, marble busts, military medals and paraphernalia, and extravagant furniture. The grounds, patterned on those of a British manor, were lined with giant cypress trees, eucalyptus, and other species of flora that had been imported to Shiwa Ng'andu.

Shiwa Ng'andu is a remote place in 2005; the road through Northern Province toward Kasama is almost impassable on occasion and throughout the 1990s was barely maintained at all. At the time of its construction in the 1920s, the house was practically inaccessible. Yet certain materials, such as windows, had to be brought over rough country by oxcart from Broken Hill (now Kabwe), some 560 kilometers (350 miles) away. Other building materials had to be produced on site, and kilns were built to fire the bricks and the

A view of the gardens and main house Shiwa Ng'andu in Northern Province, part of the estate built by Sir Stewart Gore-Browne between 1920 and 1930. Courtesy of the author.

roof tiles that formed the exterior of the massive structure as well as numerous outbuildings. In all, the estate consisted of a chapel, school, hospital, sawmill, cottages, and a store, all of which served the local Bemba community, as well as commercial operations and an energy plant based on a steam boiler. The estate depended on the production of essential oils from which to make perfumes, but it operated profitably for only a few years.

Owing to the unprofitability of this enterprise, much of the estate and surrounding area fell into deep disrepair beginning in the 1970s and 1980s. Gore-Browne's grandchildren attempted to revive the estate as a tourist operation in the 1990s, but its inaccessibility—notwithstanding a small airstrip on the grounds—and the overall weakness of Zambia's tourism industry made this doubly difficult. The house was extremely run-down from neglect and exposure to the elements by the mid-1990s; the cost of repairs was astronomical. Nevertheless, by 2001, some progress had been made. Repairing this magnificent, if wildly out of place, house may require nearly as much effort as it took to build it nearly a century ago.

The Contemporary Urban Environment of Lusaka

Some time ago, Lusaka was known as the "Garden City," in part for its broad, tree-lined avenues, carefully manicured lawns and cultivated gardens,

No longer needed to power the estate, the steam works at Shiwa Ng'andu have fallen into a state of disrepair. Courtesy of the author.

and its low, colonial-style buildings. Although much of the capital, like many of the urban centers in Zambia, has fallen into disrepair, Lusaka certainly retains a great deal of its rustic charm and overall appeal. This is reflected in the architecture of the city, which has seen both continuity and change in its new (if infrequent) development. Most recent construction in and around the capital consists of retail space and shopping malls.

The development of Lusaka, from the time the capital moved there from Livingstone in 1931, through the 1950s, was largely ad hoc. Little planning was given to African populations that remained in the city, to transport facilities, or to the spacing of commercial and residential property. It was not until the 1952 Town Planning Scheme for Lusaka that the ad hoc, scattered development that had characterized the city was consolidated into a coherent plan that would foster the "development into a town with an urban character."[6]

Commercial Buildings

Although Greater Lusaka extends some 360 square kilometers (140 square miles) and encompasses the surrounding neighborhoods and satellite townships, downtown Lusaka remains fairly small. The central business district covers less than 2 square kilometers (0.7 square mile), mostly clustered around the city's principal carriageway, Cairo Road. The industrial area lies just to the west of downtown. A number of colonial-era buildings remain in Lusaka,

This roadside store in Central Province depicts the typical architecture of postcolonial Zambia. Courtesy of the author.

mostly one- and two-story structures of unremarkable description that served as retail establishments and the administrative buildings of Northern Rhodesia. The postcolonial period, however, saw a rapid expansion in commercial construction that mirrored the growth of housing. Among the most notable postcolonial commercial architecture includes the Bank of Zambia Building, which was completed in 1975; Findeco House, finished in 1979; and the Meridien Bank Headquarters, completed in 1993. The first two structures, like the towering 20-story Zambia National Building Society House and the Industrial Development Corporation of Zambia (Indeco) House, were Zambian versions of skyscrapers and came to dominate and define the modern skyline. They, like virtually all of the big capital projects in Zambia in the 1970s, were funded by the state.

The Meridian Bank building, however, was privately constructed. It is noteworthy because it was one of few big building projects undertaken in the early 1990s, when economic conditions were particularly inauspicious. In addition, its low-lying, two-story structure mimicked that aspect of the colonial form, but it incorporated local materials and was designed to evoke traditional, rural architecture in Zambia, with its brown hues and thatchlike roof. Since the collapse of Meridien Bank, the building now houses the secretariat of the Common Market for Eastern and Southern Africa as well as other businesses.

Shortly after colonialism, most of the construction was based in central Lusaka. Among the noteworthy exceptions were the University of Zambia (built in 1967) and the Mulungushi Conference Center (built 1970), both of which lie several kilometers outside of downtown. Mulungushi was built initially to host the third summit meeting of the Non-Aligned Movement, in which Zambia's President Kaunda played a prominent role. Although it had no conference facilities at the time, in April 1970 Zambia accepted to host the summit; the building was designed and completed within four months by contractors working, literally, 24 hours a day. The final product, which can accommodate as many as 2,000 people, has held up well, despite the hastiness of its construction, although the design appears dated. Located near the parliament buildings, Mulungushi sits on several landscaped acres populated by a few gazelles and other species.

In recent years, many businesses sought to move their operations outside of the central business/government district, where traffic, parking, and, to some extent, crime create challenges for firms. Between the late 1990s and the present, the opening of shopping centers in the Makeni neighborhood, south of Lusaka, and several popular shopping centers, movie theaters, and restaurants along Great East Road, to the city's east, clearly have helped draw some commercial traffic away from town. At the same time, however, Lusaka's downtown has shown surprising resiliency; the successful refurbishment of the old Lusaka Hotel, and the opening in 2006 of a 150-plus room Protea Hotel are evidence of this.

Housing

Like any city, Lusaka consists of a diverse set of neighborhoods—among them Kabulonga, Woodlands, Kabwata, Kamwala, Avondale, Garden,

The garden and fountain at the entrance to a Zambian office building in Lusaka's Roma neighborhood reflect the variation in commercial architectural style. Courtesy of the author.

Chilenje—most of which still bear colonial-era names, which correspond with degree of wealth, power, and class. Thus, all the homes in Kabulonga, one of Lusaka's most expensive and desirable areas, are expensive, walled off by an intimidating security fence, and usually guarded by a night watchman, if not a 24-hour, security company. This is the area in which some of Zambia's wealthiest citizens reside as well as many members of the expatriate community. On the other hand, Chilenje, also in Lusaka, is a place of few paved roads, modest homes, many in a poor state of repair, and where many of the city's lower middle class and working poor reside. Kabwata is similar, except that a portion of that community is dominated by Indian homeowners, some of whom have constructed lavish two-story homes in the Indian style. Lusaka also has so-called compounds, or high-density areas. Largely appendages to city centers, these compounds were the repository for most blacks in the colonial era and remain the principal housing option for the urban poor.

The urban compounds are in many ways a vestige of colonialism.[7] Lusaka's Garden City was designed for Europeans and Asians; Africans were permitted to live in the city when employed. "African workers lived either on the property of their employer or in 'compounds' and in most cases could not be accompanied by their families. Once employment was terminated, a worker was required to leave the city and return to his village."[8] Because permanent urban settlement was deliberately discouraged in the 1930s when Lusaka began to expand, Africans' housing was rudimentary at best. Moreover,

An elite residence on the outskirts of Lusaka in Leopard's Hill. Courtesy of the author.

Northern Rhodesia's colonial planners, like their counterparts in other settler economies such as Zimbabwe and South Africa, initially made no provision for families to migrate with their husbands and fathers. This, of course, not only had an adverse impact on African family life but it also affected the type and the quality of housing available in urban compounds. Only with the promulgation of the Urban African Housing Ordinance of 1948 was a legal provision established for accommodation for Africans who were married. "It was now widely recognized that Africans might live in towns for the duration of their working lives, and be accompanied by their wives and children, but it was still assumed that on retirement they would normally return to the rural areas." This led to a rapid expansion in the number of houses, especially the construction of houses with multiple rooms.[9]

In fact, the planners miscalculated; most workers did not return to their ancestral homes at the end of their working careers. Thus, as the flow of people to the urban centers expanded, so did the amount of illegal squatting. Interestingly, this trend continued to increase and even accelerated following independence as rural Zambians pursued employment opportunities in the city. As a result, "between 1963 and 1974 ... the proportion of the city's population living in unserviced squatter areas increased from 15 percent to 42 percent."[10]

The growth in squatting notwithstanding, the arrival of independence brought substantial improvements in the number of houses and the quality of housing. In Lusaka, the government constructed so-called council housing in areas such as Chelston, Kamwala, Kabwata, Libala, and Chilenje South, which accounted for about 50 percent of the housing built in this early post-colonial period. In contrast to the compounds, such as Kalingalinga and George, these medium-density areas were preferred by people of modest income, many of whom worked for the newly independent state. The new council houses were equipped with public utilities and much better interiors. As construction of the new homes expanded, by 1970 most of the old housing, which consisted largely of thatched-roof rondavels constructed under colonial rule, was demolished. Economic downturn, which included significant worker retrenchments, has certainly altered the character of these communities over the course of three decades. Although a number of quite comfortably wealthy people reside in Chilenje and Kabwata, for example, they are a small minority within their own neighborhoods, which have suffered from the limited capacity of homeowners to reinvest in their properties and the almost total lack of government investment in infrastructure since the 1980s.

The situation is more severe in the compounds. With more than 80 percent of the population living below the poverty line, the majority of urban Zambians still live in substandard housing in crowded compounds. Squatters

A Zambian thatched cottage. © Jeremy Horner/CORBIS.

continue to reside in makeshift housing, but even the more permanent structures that occupy the compounds may lack electricity and internal plumbing, forcing households and sometimes whole communities to rely on latrines and communal water taps.

Despite these hardships, however, more amenities are more likely to be available in and around the compounds than in truly remote rural areas. In the former, even poor urban dwellers enjoy better access to transportation, communication networks and cellular phones, various forms of entertainment, and potential opportunities for work, however scarce. In the most remote rural areas, however, electricity or municipal water is often nonexistent, forcing people to rely on collecting water from natural bodies of water or from boreholes, which may be quite distant. Similarly, many continue to reside in the bamboo and mud dwellings not unlike those of a century ago. Even in the bush, as many sparsely-populated rural areas are collectively called, one occasionally finds the incongruous brick or cinder-block structure, perhaps plastered over and painted, adjacent to the 20 or 30 thatched rondavels or huts that constitute a village. As in antiquity, men are responsible for construction and thatching, whereas women do the plastering.

NOTES

1. Ellison and the Zambia National Visual Arts Council, *Art in Zambia*.
2. Teuten, *A Collector's Guide to Masks*, 39–40.

3. "Mask and Masquerade," Africa: East Africa, Grove Art Online, http://www.groveart.com/.

4. Lamb, *The Africa House,* xxvii.

5. Ibid, xxxvii.

6. Town Planning Scheme for Lusaka, Government Notice Number 300 of 1952, 3. Quoted in Collins, "Lusaka," 113.

7. This section draws on Bamberger, Sanyal, and Valverde, "Evaluation of Sites and Services Projects."

8. Collins, "Lusaka," 113.

9. Ibid., 122.

10. Bamberger, Sanyal, and Valverde, "Evaluation of Sites and Services Projects."

5

Cuisine and Traditional Dress

FOOD AND CUISINE

The history of Zambian food over the past five centuries is a history of imported tastes. Many of the foods widely available in Zambia today, some of which are even considered dietary staples—maize, cassava, rice, sweet potato, and so forth—actually originated in the Americas and were brought to Africa by traders hundreds of years ago. These crops are cultivated and consumed as so-called traditional, notwithstanding their foreign origin, revealing that food and cuisine, like culture itself, is anything but static. Indeed, consumption patterns have changed at an accelerating pace; although these crops and the foods made from them continue to be widely consumed, many contemporary Zambians increasingly consume a thoroughly Western diet. This includes some of the worst the West has to offer, such as high-fat fast food, sugar-filled drinks, and so on. In numerous shopping malls in Lusaka and other urban areas, it is possible to find Zimbabwean-based ice cream shops, South African–based chicken restaurants, U.S. sandwich chains, as well as an array of Zambian-owned enterprises. It is not surprising, therefore, that among upper-middle-class and wealthy Zambians, obesity is on the rise. The high-fat, high-carbohydrate appeal of fast food is the same as in the West: It tastes good. As an added appeal in the modernizing context of Zambia, eating from such places carries a certain cachet for many Zambians, especially young people. In short, it is considered stylish to eat pizza, burgers, and so forth and, equally, to be seen at such dining establishments.

Thus, food is not unlike other aspects of traditional Zambian culture and customs: It is being altered in significant ways. In some important respects, the long-standing traditional diet has been eroded in favor of that which is more akin to Western style. Yet it is important not to overstate the spread of this phenomenon or of national waistlines. First of all, even wealthy urbanites continue to eat the traditional foods of their forebears, though this may be infrequent in some families. Moreover, although the urban elite class has the wherewithal to purchase Western-style food, whether prepared in a restaurant or in the home, the vast majority of Zambians remain desperately poor; particularly in recent years marred by drought, many do not even have access to adequate food at all. Impoverished Zambians, both rural and urban, therefore, stick largely to the traditional diet. On the whole, traditional cuisine can be quite healthful, but in the prevailing socioeconomic climate—not to mention the natural one—the typical meal for most Zambians is likely to be quite simple and probably insufficiently nutritious. Dinner at one of Lusaka's fine restaurants, food from the ubiquitous takeaways (take-out stands), or even a fully stocked pantry are almost unimaginable luxuries to a majority of Zambians.

Traditional Zambian Diets

The one food item likely found on the dining tables of all Zambians, regardless of class, wealth, or ethnicity, is *nshima,* a stiff dough or dumpling, of sorts, made from ground corn (maize meal, referred to as mealie meal). Although the etymology of the word lies in Zambia's Eastern Province, there are regional variants: Lozis, for example, know it as *buhobe,* Bembas as *ubwali,* and so on, but virtually all Zambians refer to this staple food as *nshima.* It is believed that maize (corn) was first introduced to Africa by the Portuguese sometime around the fifteenth century, although it did not reach Zambian populations until the late eighteenth century. Moreover, although their cultivation was fairly widespread, neither maize nor the other North American and nonindigenous crops such as sweet potatoes, groundnuts, and cassava "were regarded as 'real food' by the Bembas at this time."[1] Centuries later, *nshima* is consumed not only by Zambians but also by Kenyans and Tanzanians (where it is known as *ugali),* Zimbabweans *(sadza),* South Africans *(pap),* and others throughout eastern and southern Africa.

Nshima is prepared by grinding milled corn into a fine meal. Throughout Zambia, even the smallest plots support maize plants, although already ground mealie meal is typically distributed or purchased ground and sold in bags of various quantities, from 5 kilograms to 40 kilograms. *Nshima* is prepared by vigorously mixing this meal with boiling water over a hot stove or fire. The cooked *nshima* is scooped from the pot using a large wooden cooking stick (more like a paddle or large spoon) and served piping hot by rounded spoonfuls about the size of a large potato. Like many traditional Zambian foods, *nshima* is eaten without utensils; using the fingers and palm of one hand, one kneads a small piece of *nshima* into the proper shape to be used to dip into or scoop up accompanying foods, which most people refer to as relish. This relish *(ndiwo)* is, ideally, a mixture of meat and vegetables, or at least gravy of some kind. *Nshima,* the rather bland taste of which bears a slight resemblance to unflavored grits or farina, is nearly always eaten with this relish (preferably including meat), which completes the meal. What Zambians call relish would probably be seen as the main course in most Western cultures, but its status as a second dish in Zambia illustrates the central importance of *nshima* to the daily meal. It is not uncommon for Zambians to eat two meals with *nshima* each day, although in times of personal and/or national hardship, this may be reduced to one or even fewer. Similarly, only in times of hardship would *nshima* be consumed without relish.

Among other common traditional vegetables and side dishes are millet, cassava (manioc), groundnuts, various leaves (pumpkin, sweet potato, cassava), beans, a collard green–type vegetable called rape, and various kinds of local mushrooms. The typical method of preparation is to finely chop these vegetables and boil them in water and cook them in oil with onions and tomatoes. Groundnuts (peanuts) are also ground into peanut butter and mixed with prepared vegetables, such as spinach or cabbage.

Besides *nshima,* other starches include rice, potatoes and sweet potatoes, and yams. Finger millet was the preferred staple in the nineteenth century, although it is much less popular today, despite its suitability for Zambian agricultural conditions. Also less commonly eaten is sorghum, which is a grasslike plant native to Zambia, but sorghum, like cassava, is a vital drought-hardy crop that plays an important role in diets, especially in times of scarce rains when food security becomes paramount.

A number of fruits are found in Zambia and enjoy great popularity. These include pawpaw (papaya), mango, lemons, and bananas. Also plentiful are groundnuts, which are cultivated, and avocados, both of which are among the many nonindigenous plants that now grow in many parts of the country and provide important supplements to the traditional diet. The horticulture industry expanded in Zambia in the 1990s to produce a far wider variety of fruits and vegetables, though this type of farming, which is capital-intensive and requires irrigation and sometimes hothouses, has increasingly set its sights on more lucrative export markets, rather than local consumers, for their high-end produce.

In urban environments, beef, chicken, and pork are commonly found in the supermarkets; however, these items are fairly unusual in rural households. Meat is a luxury item for most Zambians, particularly in the rural areas, even among Zambia's more than 600,000 subsistence farmers who might possess a few goats and chickens. In general, because of their substantial expense, large farm animals such as cows, pigs, or even goats and sheep are slaughtered only on special occasions, including weddings and ceremonies, among poor Zambians, even those who may own such animals. Moreover, cows provide a critical source of milk and manure, so they have value outside of their meat. Those farming on a larger scale, and certainly most commercial farmers, have poultry, pigs, and cows, although in some parts of the country, like Northern Province, cows are uncommon except in relatively sophisticated farming operations that have dip tanks, because of the prevalence of the tsetse fly. Zambia's Southern Province is far more suitable to cattle ranching, and the Tonga people are renowned cattle farmers.

Zambia's myriad lakes and rivers contribute to a diet that tends to be rich in fish, although, interestingly, most ethnic groups do not have a strong fishing tradition. The Lozi people, however, are considered to have a fish-heavy diet, probably due to their proximity to the Zambezi River. Similarly, communities such as Mpulungu, the town bordering Lake Tanganyika in Northern Province, are largely based on fishing for their livelihood. Native and nonnative species are abundant in Zambia's waters, including everything from larger sport fish such as Nile perch and tiger fish, to tilapia (bream) and the tiny *kapenta,* which measures just a few millimeters in length. Each group has its own methods for catching fish, which may include the use of baskets, barbed spears, and the temporary obstruction of rivers. Preparation methods also vary according to ethnic traditions. Although perhaps the preferred

A commercial farm in Central Province has sufficient resources for cattle raising. Courtesy of the author.

method of preparation is to cook fish along with a stew of vegetables, as with the meat dishes described previously, dried fish is also popular, partly given the potentially long distances between catch and consumption. The minnow-size *kapenta,* for example, is always dried and eaten whole, partially resaturated with a tomato-based sauce and *nshima.*

Many Zambians do not share Western, or at least U.S., aversions to dining on various kinds of insects and rodents, such as mice, although these tastes vary greatly by ethnic group and by region. Among the Bemba and other groups, for example, large caterpillars are considered something of a delicacy: Dried, fried in oil, and eaten as a side dish, these abundant creatures make a tasty snack known as *ifikubala.* In addition, grasshoppers, known as *icipaso* in iciBemba, are prepared in a similar way. In Eastern Province, especially among the Tumbuka, mice, gutted and properly cooked, are a popular food. It should be noted that the culinary attractiveness of mice does not necessarily extend to other rodents; rats, for example, are not eaten and are seen as dirty and disease-ridden.

Beverages

Despite Zambia's abundant waterways, potable water is scarce in the country. This is the result of human pollution, due to direct and indirect discharge of waste into the waterways, as well as naturally occurring waterborne pathogens. Consequently, although water is perhaps the most commonly consumed beverage throughout the country, it must be boiled first to be genuinely safe for consumption. Even in town and city water supplies, which are fed by reservoirs through pipes, and a generally adequate sewer system, water must first be boiled before drinking to eliminate the risk of cholera and other diseases, which see occasional outbreaks. Bottled water, including a local brand sold under the name Manzi ("water" in Nyanja), is available in most urban areas, but the cost of treated bottled water is prohibitive for most Zambians.

Colonialism introduced tea to Africa, and today the beverage is ubiquitous in Zambia, where it is also grown in small quantities. Zambians also drink coffee, although it is not nearly as popular as tea among the British-influenced populace. Interestingly, coffee is a crop that has been promoted by exporters but has a scant domestic following. Tea or coffee are taken following meals or at meetings, breaks, and so on. Hosts are expected to serve tea to their visitors, whether before or after the meal, and most Zambians enjoy it with a large dose of sugar and milk, in the English style.

With a strong foothold in Africa, Coca-Cola is also ubiquitous, and Coke and its sister brands are found in even the most remote and unlikeliest of locations throughout Zambia. Available throughout Africa for decades, Coke products are locally bottled and distributed throughout the country. Because it is produced in

Zambia, Coke, Sprite, and so on tend to be relatively cheap, perhaps around 30 cents a bottle, but as with all other consumer goods in contemporary Zambia, the poor would nevertheless see this as a luxury item to be consumed occasionally, rather than a daily beverage. Moreover, it is somewhat unusual, even among urban elites, to see Coke drunk with meals, fast food excepted.

Alcoholic beverages, ranging from traditional home brews to domestically produced beer to imported liquors, are also popular in Zambia. The so-called home brews made from finger millet—such as the mildly fermented *katata* and *katubi* of the Bemba, served with an *nsupa* (calabash)—were once quite common in the rural areas, but they have been substantially replaced in many parts of Zambia by packaged beverages. The commercially manufactured Chibuku (referred to throughout Zambia as Shake-Shake), which comes in a milk-style carton, is a thick, traditional-style opaque beer. It is also cheaper than bottled beer and thus appeals to many drinkers on the basis of price. The large so-called clear-beer industry boasts a number of familiar Zambian brands, such as Rhino and Mosi, as well as South African imports such as the Castle brand. In fact, Zambia Breweries and Northern Breweries, the makers of Mosi and Rhino, respectively, have been owned for nearly a decade by South African Breweries, whose Castle is now joined by a host of globally recognized brands, including Miller beer. It is a reflection of the importance of status—an air of cosmopolitanism—as well as Zambians' changing tastes that many urban Zambians prefer the familiar South African brands to Zambian brews, despite the fact that they are all produced by the same company. Beer and other alcoholic beverages can be imbibed at home, although most Zambians, urban as well as rural, more often tend to go to a local club, shebeen, or bar to drink. Few if any prohibitions prevent women going to bars and clubs, although a clear stigma is attached to those who go unaccompanied. By and large, in keeping with gender roles, married women are expected to stay home with the children when and if their husbands go out drinking.

The Environmental Impact of Food Consumption

Wild game, including various antelope species, birds, and occasionally large animals such as elephants, once formed a critical source of meat protein through the early twentieth century. Restrictions on the hunting of certain game animals, such as elephants, may be largely ignored, but in fact these creatures are today scarce outside of Zambia's protected national parks. Even there, some big game animals, such as the rhinoceros, have been hunted nearly to extinction, although more by poachers than by people looking to kill rhino, or other endangered species, for meat. Only the city of Livingstone's Mosi-oa-Tunya National Park is fully fenced; elsewhere, animals that migrate outside park boundaries are likely to be killed by hunters or by farmers protecting fields and livestock. Indeed, one is struck when driving through remote, sparsely inhabited regions of Zambia's Northern Province, for example, at the absence of wildlife, both large and small. Thus, the creation of the 19 national parks and, more importantly, the overhunting of certain species have reduced the amount of game meat any group would actually eat.

Zambian commercial farmers are fond of saying that their country should be the breadbasket of the region. In fact, Zambia is a net importer of food, which has become increasingly expensive, and subsistence production is highly dependent on an unpredictable climate. Moreover, the paucity of game in rural areas and the rising expense of farm-raised sources of meat such as beef and pork have contributed to a reemphasis on other traditional items made of cheaper and, for the moment, at least, more plentiful ingredients, although this, too, has consequences, as discussed later.

One such popular food, known as *chikanda* among the Bemba and *chinaka* among Nyanja-speakers, is also referred to as "African baloney" because of its shape, consistency, and color. Long associated with special occasions, this traditional dish made from orchid tubers, chili, groundnuts, salt, and baking soda has experienced renewed popularity in recent years among Zambia's urban dwellers. Today it is served both as part of traditional ceremonies and, increasingly, regular meals because it is far cheaper than meat. The trend has a dangerous downside, however. The high demand for and popularity of chinaka has led to intense orchid harvesting; up to 85 species are facing rapid depletion and possibly extinction. Indeed, "more than 2.2 million wild orchids are being strip-mined each year because of the growing demand to use them as food."[2] Furthermore, recent research suggests that a number of traditional vegetable species in Zambia face similar "threats of extinction due to land clearing for agriculture, urbanization and overgrazing," and conservation efforts have had only marginal impact.[3]

In short, a variety of animal and plant species face threats, some severe, as the ripple effects of poverty, food shortages, and environmental stresses affect the Zambian populace, particularly in rural areas. The return to traditional food items or the greater reliance on certain foods, some of which like *chikanda* are considered delicacies, is being driven as much out of desperation as by cultural renaissance. Such trends threaten to create vicious circles in which greater scarcity results.

Everyday and Ceremonial Meal Preparation

The vast majority of Zambian meals served in the home are prepared by women and girls. Indeed, although extreme, some tales suggest it is even bad luck for a man to handle a woman's cooking stick, the implement used most typically for making *nshima*. Mothers or wives will serve all meals in the home, perhaps with assistance from a domestic worker in the case of a well-off urban family, although young unmarried men would be expected to fend for themselves at mealtime.

A basic breakfast generally consists of bread or porridge, usually made of maize, together with tea. Eggs are also abundant and inexpensive, whereas Western-style breakfast cereals are also on the rise in urban households. Lunch often consists of *nshima* with one or more of the relishes described previously, the type and variety of these supporting dishes determined by the wealth of the diner. In the home, dinner may consist of any leftover relish from lunchtime, although, almost invariably, *nshima* will be made fresh with each meal. Indeed, something of a ritual surrounds the preparation and distribution of *nshima* in the household, and it is considered ill-mannered to serve someone leftover *nshima*. In traditional practice, hands are washed at the table (in the

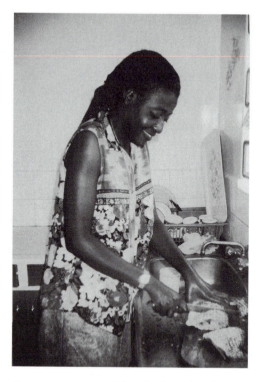

A woman prepares fish, which is abundant in Zambia's rivers and lakes. Courtesy of the author.

past, in a common bowl; today, usually with soap as water is poured from a pitcher held over the bowl). The washing of hands, like the serving of food, is based on seniority and gender. The father will be served first, unless there is a male guest in the home, who then takes precedence. Thereafter comes any senior guests, the family matriarch, and so on. The children are served last. It is worth noting that even many of these norms are eroding among Westernized families within cities like Lusaka.

Food and the preparation of food play central roles in a number of traditional ceremonies. The Bemba *amatebeto,* also discussed in chapter 6, is part of the marriage ritual in which the female relatives of the bride prepare a feast for the groom and his family. Typically offered in the weeks before the actual wedding, the *amatebeto* requires the female members of the bridal party to prepare all the traditional foods, which are then brought to the groom's residence. The preparation is marked by singing, stories, and camaraderie at the home of the bride's mother. The foods, both exotic and familiar, are presented one by one—chicken, *chikanda, ifikubala,* the list is extensive—and it is explained that these foods are those that the bride herself will later prepare as part of her wifely duties. The Bemba *ukwingisha shifyala,* which may take place many years following the wedding, also involves food. Because the *ukwingisha shifyala* marks the symbolic acceptance of the son-in-law into the family, it is celebrated with food; he brings his family to his wife's mother's home for a meal. According to tradition, he is not allowed to dine with his mother-in-law prior to that time.

Various traditional dishes are presented at the *amatebeto* ceremony. Courtesy of the author.

A food-centered celebration that involves not only an extended family but also the entire community is the Nc'wala, or first fruits ceremony, of the Ngoni people in Eastern Province. Held in February, the Nc'wala commemorates the arrival in Zambia of the Ngoni, one of the few Zambian ethnic groups to arrive from the south, in the 1830s. The first produce of the year's harvest is sampled by the chief, who presides over a ceremony that includes, in addition to food, considerable drink as well as traditional dances.

Buying Food, Growing Food, and Food Aid

Markets and Shops

In almost all Zambian cities and towns, most foods can be purchased at a supermarket. Several large grocery chains, dominated, as is much of Zambia's private sector since the 1990s, by South African firms, occupy Zambia's major cities. These stores are virtually indistinguishable from the Western prototype: characterized by large, well-lit aisles, extensive food selection, a range of nonfood items for sale, and a long bank of registers at the checkout counter. Middle-class families residing in major towns like Lusaka, Ndola, or Kitwe, for example, buy the majority of their food at the supermarket, although they will often go to the open-air or specialty markets to buy fish, vegetables, and maize meal, where items are more easily inspected and prices

Many Zambians purchase their goods and produce at outdoor markets like this one. Courtesy of the author.

Although inefficient, the *citemene* system of slash-and-burn agriculture is an ancient practice. Courtesy of the author.

are usually negotiable. Impoverished citizens especially find the prices at the large stores prohibitive, and the markets provide a more practical location to purchase smaller quantities of food. Zambians dwelling in the rural areas, however, are much more likely to be involved in subsistence—that is, production for their own consumption—although only in the smallest, most remote settlements will no retail shop of any kind be found. Even in such places, however, one is likely to find items for sale, such as modest surplus of fruits, vegetables, and so forth, usually by the roadside, assuming one exists.

Food Production

The geography of Zambia is quite varied. The lands of Southern and Central Provinces, with altitudes from 3,000 feet to 5,000 feet at Zambia's central plateau and adequate rainfalls, tend to support the most diverse agriculture. Given its favorable soils, climate, topography, and access to water, what is today Zambia's Southern Province attracted large-scale commercial farming during the colonial period. A number of these farms continue to be operated by white farmers. The Tonga, who are the dominant group within Southern Province, have long excelled at raising cattle. Although they were pushed into subsistence agriculture during that period, many Tonga are today involved in medium- and large-scale commercial farming activities.

In contrast, the soils of Northern Province, where Bemba speakers predominate, are generally poor and, therefore, not well suited to agriculture. The climate and topography are not particularly suitable to the keeping of cattle, either, absent substantial intervention by contemporary veterinary medicine, which itself requires considerable resources. This is not to suggest, however, that the Bemba and other groups have not attempted to farm or that cows are not found in Zambia's north; on the contrary. Rather, it is an issue instead of return, yield, and efficiency (indeed, there is a reason that the inhabitants of this region were primarily hunting cultures in antiquity). The type of agriculture practiced by most groups in the northern part of Zambia continues to be the highly inefficient slash-and-burn form, called *chitemene,* or *citemene* in iciBemba, a method that has been prevalent in the region at least since the seventeenth century. After existing woodland is burned, the nitrogen-rich ash supports the cultivation of millet, groundnuts, beans, and cassava, but only for about four or five years, then the soil lies fallow for 20 to 30 years. Obviously, coupled with population pressures, this form of cultivation is highly destructive to habitat and forestland. Moreover, it has been "estimated that the chitemene system could support between 2 and 4 persons per square kilometer depending on the amount of suitable land available."[4] Not only is this totally inadequate in modern times, "For most families, there is an annual period of shortage, if not actual famine, during the later part of the rainy season (January to March) before the new crop is ready for harvest."[5] In short, for a significant percentage of Zambia's populace, traditional farming methods simply do not yield sufficient quantities of food to support communities.

The Need for Food Aid

In response to pressure from the World Bank, the International Monetary Fund, the donor community, as well as domestic forces, Zambia substantially liberalized its agricultural markets in the 1990s. Although similar efforts had failed in the 1980s, the more sustained effort in the 1990s left obsolete a vast state marketing board bureaucracy. Whereas this reduced demands on government budgets, the demise of the marketing boards that had bought, sold, transported, and distributed agricultural produce meant that many small-scale farmers were left without access to inputs or markets. Instead of stimulating the agricultural sector, then, liberalization brought it to the brink of collapse.

Of course, in a well-functioning market, residents of Zambia's less fertile regions would be able to purchase or import food produced elsewhere in the country. For a variety of reasons, however, using a market-based approach to food distribution in Zambia has not been effective. For example, far-flung areas simply are not efficient to supply because of the expense. (This is the same reason private transport companies refuse to service farmers in these areas as well: because it is unprofitable for them to do so.) At the same time, rural poverty is too entrenched to afford to purchase food from outside and so on.

In response to these worsening economic conditions and the frequency of drought in the region in the 1990s, the Zambian government established a Food Reserve Agency (FRA). Intended to meet food needs, particularly in times of drought, the FRA's record has been mixed. Instead, in recent years many poor Zambians have been dependent on food aid from the donor community. This has not been without considerable controversy itself, however. For example, in 2002, Zambia experienced its fourth drought in a decade and faced looming food shortages. The donors offered food aid, although the United States, the leading source of food relief, insisted that its relief be in the form of GMO (genetically modified organism) maize. Concerned about threats to health and to the environment, Zambia rejected GMO food aid from the United States. Later in 2002, the government banned all importation of GMO products, despite outrage in the United States that Zambia was literally biting the hand that attempted to feed it.

It is unclear whether Zambia can block GMO from entering the food chain; indeed, it is a near certainty that some GMO seed has already penetrated Zambia on at least a limited scale. Other countries import GMO, and in South Africa approximately 20 percent of the national maize and wheat crop is now GMO. Given Zambia's reliance on South Africa and the presence of so many South African firms in Zambia—South African Breweries and Shoprite Checkers among them—it is unclear if the country will be able to insulate its population from any ill effects, real or potential, from GMO. Moreover, in some ways the rejection of GMO is at odds with the increasingly Western orientation of the Zambian diet, at least that of elites. It is unclear to what degree Zambian elites worry about the healthfulness of their food. Nor is it clear if poor rural Zambians are as concerned about GMO as is their government or whether they are simply focused more directly on access to food, period, regardless of its provenance.

TRADITIONAL DRESS

Women in Zambia are frequently clad in colorful printed cloth known as *chitenge*. These rectangular-shaped *chitenge* are wrapped around the waist as skirts or sarongs; smaller, matching pieces may be used as head scarves; and in some cases, the cloth may be sewn into a top that complements the other components. Shirts, pants, and vests made of *chitenge* are also quite common. *Chitenge* is an affordable fabric and nearly ubiquitous in Zambia.

Two examples of fashionable clothing made from *chitenge* cloth. Courtesy of the author.

During election years, it is not uncommon to see a proliferation of *chitenge* bearing the images of leading politicians and candidates, and these political advertisements thus become embedded in fashion. Scaling up the ladder of wealth, from poorer rural women to wealthier urban counterparts, it is possible to see increasingly lavish designs in *chitenge* or other cloth. Indeed, it is not uncommon in Lusaka, for example, to see women of some means wearing beautifully designed, expertly tailored *chitenge* ensembles for everyday use. Because the fabric is inexpensive, lightweight, and versatile, it is an African alternative to Western fashion. For more formal occasions, women especially will often wear African-themed prints and embroidery. In these fashions, one finds skirts and tops and head scarves as well as larger robes made from two pieces of square cloth with a hole cut for the head and cinched and stitched under the arms, similar to the West African boubou. Frequently, these are made from fabrics heavier and sturdier than *chitenge,* which is no more rigid than a handkerchief. Whereas this style of clothing is distinctively African—the patterns, the colors, the textures, and the styles are quite recognizable as inspired by African tradition—there is little that is uniquely Zambian about it.

In fact, the colorful, often exotic patterns are borrowed from other African cultures and traditions. The boubou itself is a West African garment worn by women and men and is found in Senegal, Nigeria, and elsewhere. The *chitenge* prints began to appear widely as a staple of Zambian clothing not in some bygone, precolonial era but in the 1960s; indeed, the early influences spread to Zambia from the neighboring Democratic Republic of the Congo as well as from other parts of West Africa. The 1960s and early 1970s, particularly the years immediately preceding and following independence, were a time of great African nationalism. Although by no means universal, a significant continental consciousness emerged. Among many elites, this was reflected in politics and culture as well as fashion and included a rejection of exclusively Western attire and its supplementation (if not exactly replacement) with African traditional clothing, or at least clothing inspired by traditional styles. In Zambia, however, this proved somewhat problematic, as the country lacked any easily identifiable garb—certainly not one with broad national appeal— or even a tradition of fashion.

Indeed, traditional dress in Zambia lacks the distinctive and familiar styles found in many other parts of Africa, such as Ghanaian kente cloth, with its rich textures and vital ceremonial role; the simplicity of Kenyan *kanga* cloth; or the elegant robes, whether in vibrant color or simply white, of West African countries like Senegal and Nigeria. In Zambia, there is no national costume, and generally there is only a narrow range of designs and styles— that is, limited variation—among the country's 73 ethnolinguistic groups.

Perhaps the most distinctive articles of traditional dress among Zambian communities is the *musisi,* the traditional costume worn by Lozi women. It consists of a large skirt that extends from the waist in a conical shape. An internal frame enables the *musisi* to retain its shape when worn, although it is not so rigid to prevent the whole enterprise from moving during traditional dances. Yet the *musisi* appears no more likely to be adopted or recognized as the national costume than any other less distinctive representation. In fact, at the United Nations' Fourth World Conference on Women, held in Beijing in 1995, members of the Zambian delegation thought it appropriate to attend the opening ceremonies of the conference in national dress. Even this small the group was unable to agree on the *musisi,* however, in part because of its singular identification with Lozi traditions. Because virtually all other clothing lacked a particular ethnic distinctiveness, the idea was abandoned.

Elsewhere in Zambia, prior to the arrival of colonialism, traditional dress consisted mainly of animal skins or bark cloth wrapped around the waist or draped over the shoulders much like a Roman toga. Some animal skins are still worn in traditional ceremonies. Cotton textile weaving was not part of precolonial Zambian cultures, except in the Zambezi River valley and in the northeast, and once European clothing styles were introduced to Zambia, they permeated virtually all of the communities quite quickly. Thus, for men in particular, trousers rapidly became part of the clothing repertoire, and contemporary male fashion in Zambia is unambiguously Western at all income levels and across all subcultures.

Some contemporary Western-style clothes were made in Zambia, but with the collapse of the state-owned clothing and textile sector in the 1990s, production was severely curtailed. As incomes declined and sources of domestically produced clothing shrank, Zambians turned increasingly toward *salaula,* or secondhand clothing. Meaning "to pick from a pile" or "rummaging," *salaula,* or simply, *sally,* has become an important source of clothing for many urban Zambians. Even those of some means will choose from among the suits, dresses, T-shirts, and so on offered for sale at a fraction of the cost of new clothing. This clothing, nearly always of good quality, arrives in bulk containers, usually donated from Western countries. Although secondhand clothes have been imported to Zambia for decades, the market for *salaula* increased markedly in the late 1980s and 1990s, corresponding with the widening economic crisis in the country.

NOTES

1. Roberts, *A History of the Bemba,* 210–11.
2. "Eaten as Food, African Orchids Threatened by Illegal Trade."
3. Mingochi and Luchen, "Traditional Vegetables in Zambia."
4. Mathews, "Chitemene, Fundikila and Hybrid Farming."
5. Roberts, *A History of the Bemba,* xxvii.

6

Gender Roles, Marriage, and Family

It has been said in some circles that African women are the most oppressed group of people on earth. Although such a claim is difficult to substantiate in a scientific manner, African women do tend to be poorer, of lesser social status, more vulnerable to disease, and shorter-lived than their female counterparts elsewhere in the world. Certainly, African women have faced enormous obstacles, hardships, and discrimination within the family, community, state, and international context relative to males. They have made remarkable strides in some countries—in the areas of women's rights, inheritance laws, political participation and representation, and business ownership, to name a few—but, for the most part, the world in which most African women reside remains firmly dominated by men.

In considering gender relations in Africa, Zambia represents something of a middle case; its politics, economics, culture, and traditions continue to assign often fixed and typically subordinate roles to women, yet women have made gains in each of these areas as well. Moreover, as in other sub-Saharan African countries, the collision of the traditional with the modern or Western, first via colonialism and more contemporarily through globalization and the various media described in chapter 3, has had a contradictory effect. On the one hand, colonialism brought conservative forces (Christianity, rigid gender roles), and on the other hand, Western culture more recently has brought global feminism and its attendant pressures to change local gender hierarchies and cultural norms. As everywhere else, these competing norms continue to exist in tension with one another.

This chapter places women in a wider discourse about gender roles, marriage, and family relations in Zambia. Importantly, the interest in gender is distinct from a chapter on women. Whereas the discussion of gender inevitably leads back to the status of women in society, it is impossible to address gender roles without also considering the position, status, and power of men in Zambian society. Although women and men have distinct roles as well as a number of shared roles and responsibilities as coequals, in the majority of contexts women are but a mirror image, a relatively powerless reflection of their male counterparts. In short, all aspects of life—family, social, economic, and legal—in Zambia and in Africa in general are simply harder for women than they are for men. This has wider implications beyond issues of fairness. Indeed, this reality suggests that Zambia has a long way to go; the uplift of more than 50 percent of its citizens is imperative to improve not only the lives of women but the broader development prospects of the country as a whole.

Women were always regarded as inferior to men in Zambia, even before the coming of the colonial powers. (It is important not to overstate the precolonial harmonious gender relations, women's empowerment, etc., although, to some degree, this was true in other countries.) Nonetheless, a number of powers were available to women or a woman's family. These were altered by colonialism and the arrival of Christianity, which diminished the role of the bride/wife while elevating the role of the father/husband. It also imported a Victorian ideal about the position of women (ironic, given that Victoria herself made it to queen!) and the subservient position vis-à-vis men and husbands.

Women generally have lower status in traditional rural environments as well as in contemporary urban contexts. In rural areas, many young men are still drawn to the cities, as they were in colonial times, although this rural-to-urban migration was particularly acute in the colonial period. Recall that Zambia's principal contribution t to the colonial enterprise was its copper ore and mining capacity. Considerable amounts of unskilled and semiskilled black labor were needed in the mines, which were located in the Central and Copperbelt Provinces. Invariably, men were recruited, at times forcibly, to these tasks, leaving many rural regions devoid of working-age males. Although today the mining industry in Zambia operates at a fraction of its colonial peak production, the gender imbalances prompted by rural-to-urban migration patterns continue, prompted by the promise of employment. Thus, one often finds that in rural areas there are more women than men. Women then assume primary responsibility for maintaining the home and for subsistence.

POLITICS AND POWER

National Roles

The start of the twenty-first century sees many advances as well as stubborn holdovers from the past. In short, gender relations in contemporary Zambia are characterized by a series of contradictions. For example, today women are found in politics and positions of power. Women own businesses, run nongovernmental organizations, and occupy all the professions; few, if any, avenues are presumptively foreclosed to women on the basis of gender. Yet considerable obstacles still remain to their attaining equality with men. Some are supply-based: Fewer educated or wealthy women are poised to assume positions in government or business, for instance. Poverty has had a particularly devastating impact on girls and women. The girl child is educated last and often married first, perhaps as young as age 13.

Further, women have yet to access politics at nearly the same level as men. Although women participate actively in the new democratic structures in Zambia, few go on to win positions in the National Assembly, Zambia's parliament. On the other hand, women have been appointed to key government ministries, including health, finance, agriculture, and the ambassadorship to the United States. Yet Zambia lags well behind many other African countries, including South Africa, Mozambique, Rwanda, and Uganda, in terms of women's political representation. Indeed, among Zambia's southern African neighbors, South Africa and Mozambique have guaranteed, reserved seats for women in parliament and, as a result, have more than 30 percent of their legislative seats occupied by women; Zambia, with no such requirement, has only 20 women in its 150-member parliament. Considering the substantial burdens on women, both as political candidates and as members of Zambian society, they are likely to remain a small percentage of the legislators absent proactive attempts to increase the number of female officeholders. Similar gender imbalances obtain at lower levels of government (although it must be noted, these are generally weak in centralized Zambia). In substantially rural provinces, such as North Western, women occupy positions in the formal political realm as headmen, chiefs, and local government officials only rarely.[1] Finally, one woman, Gwendolyn Konie, ran for president in 2001. Although she lost overwhelmingly, she set an important symbolic precedent, and others, including the outspoken Edith Nawakwi of the Forum for Development and Democracy (FDD) party, have indicated that they intend to run in the future.

Community and Family Roles

Males and females approach daily life quite differently. Girls and women in cities like Lusaka are responsible for cleaning house and doing the laundry and cooking. In rural areas, to these tasks are added looking after children, gathering water and firewood, and engaging in subsistence farming. Boys may have a narrower set of chores and will often be found playing football (soccer)—a ubiquitous sport in Zambia. Men cultivate fields in rural communities or work elsewhere. In both rural and urban environments, men are less likely to work around the house when they are through with their wage-earning activities. Men, therefore, typically, will sit together and talk, play games together, and perhaps drink beer together, if they have access to it. Few cultural prohibitions in Zambia prevent men engaging in what may be regarded—in some countries and among some cultures—as women's work, such as doing laundry and cooking. Nonetheless, it would be uncommon to see a male performing these chores if he has a wife or female relative around. Although the colonial government compelled many able-bodied males into the wage economy, including into the mining sector as labor, it also introduced cash-cropping to many rural areas. Thus, men became responsible for cash crops—and claimed the revenue they generated—whereas women remained in control over subsistence, that is, the household and production.

Women carrying heavy loads, such as these bags of maize on their heads and children on their backs, is a familiar sight throughout Zambia. Courtesy of Megan Simon Thomas (2005).

The introduction of income (which accrued to the husband) and this new division of labor fostered a degree of competition in the household that did not exist previously and also served to harden gender roles that persist today.

Both male and female household roles are in addition to any employment held, although wealthier, urban-based Zambians typically employ workers to look after the household chores and the gardening. For poorer Zambians, family life and obligations are similar whether in the urban or rural parts of the country, except that people living in cities may have a wider range of social and employment opportunities. In general, therefore, life is far harder for Zambians living in far-flung, underserved areas of the country. The comparative ease of city life should not be overstated, however, because poor infrastructure and chronic unemployment characterize Zambia's impoverished urban compounds.

Certainly, one's sex defines certain roles and imposes limitations, particularly since the dawn of colonialism. In all Zambian cultures, however, age is a more important status marker than gender. Zambia, like most African countries, operates on gerontocratic principles; that is, age is supposed to be respected, even revered. Whereas position in the household or community is also a determining factor in one's status in society, age tends to stand out above other identifiers. As a result, older women, whether mothers, grandmothers, or mothers-in-law, are always expected to command respect. Girls and younger women always defer to elders; thus, when a daughter or daughter-in-law enters the presence of her mother (or mother-in-law), in some traditions, she should kneel, never stand. In fact, many traditions dictate that she should also refrain from eye contact with her elder. Younger men are expected to treat elder women with the same reverence, although some of the details of their interaction would differ from female-to-female interchange. It is worth noting, however, that these customs have been relaxed in many contemporary settings—failing to make eye contact or kneeling in a professional context, for example, would be, at best, impractical and often inappropriate—but are typically preserved in informal, family environments.

It is also important to point out the limits to gerontocratic practices. Notably, although older women are accorded respect due their age, this does not tend to improve their position in the overall gender hierarchy, which remains male-dominated. Thus, barring physical disability, even an older woman would typically be expected to serve the man first, see to his needs, and, in some cases, kneel before her husband; women are nearly always subordinate to men. Even if an elderly woman becomes a widow, the status accorded to her late husband is assumed by another man, probably a senior male relative of the deceased.

MARRIAGE AND MARITAL EXPECTATIONS

Marriage is a vital part of gender relations and identity. Historically, it was rare to see adults who had never been married, and marriage remains an important aspect of manhood and womanhood. In marriage, women are too often regarded as the so-called junior partner, which manifests itself in a number of ways. In a literal sense, girls are married younger than males, and many of these may become mothers at around age 15, although in urban areas, with greater access to education and other opportunities, both are rather uncommon. Chapter 50 of the Marriage Act stipulates that a person less than 21 years of age requires written consent of a parent or guardian to marry. The act, however, does not apply to marriages entered into under customary law, which in fact permits child marriages as long as the child (almost always a girl) has reached puberty. Although this, too, is subject to parental consent (not the formalized written consent, which is a legal document), it results in girls as young as 12 or 13 being married off by their families. It is easy to see that girls in this situation then lose not only their access to education and a chance at autonomy but childhood itself.

Women's junior or subordinate status is also revealed in the practice of polygyny, or the taking of multiple wives. In the pre-Christian period, polygyny was common among most groups, although in contemporary Zambia, partly owing to the inculcation of Christian mores, the practice is generally frowned upon; the Tonga people are perhaps its most frequent practitioners. Cultural relativists emphasize the logic of polygyny for agrarian peoples. Indeed, one study of the Tonga of the Monze region argues that polygyny was very common. Once the new household had been established, "the man had the right to look for a second wife. The first wife would not object to this because polygyny was considered as a social security. More children meant that at least some would survive to perform the family sacrifices [obligations]. Secondly, the man was not supposed to sleep with his pregnant wife. Thirdly, more wives would mean more hands for work in the maize and vegetable fields."[2]

Yet sensitivity to non-Western cultures, however laudable, should not blind us to the fact that the practice discriminates against women. Moreover, although formal polygyny is less common today in Zambia, the social attitudes that sustained polygyny remain prevalent. Recent research argues that women actually idealize the notion of monogamy and faithfulness in marriage, suggesting that they, too, find the polygyny disheartening, if not anachronistic.[3] Yet rather than taking additional wives, per se, many simply take on numerous girlfriends and sexual partners. Indeed, husbands often expect to keep a girlfriend on the side. This is such a commonly accepted practice, in fact, that one can regularly see even prominent, married men out at night with their female companions; such encounters inevitably become something of an open secret in the community. It is also not uncommon that the girlfriends will have children or possibly contract the HIV virus that causes AIDS. Interestingly enough, whereas those wives who endure wayward husbands do not exactly condone their extramarital relationships, there is often a sense of resignation expressed simply as "that is what men do." Ironically, in this age of HIV and AIDS, it is less risky to have multiple sex partners in the context of a polygynous marriage than it is between unmarried partners.

In sum, the Zambian approach to marriage is paradoxical. Whereas marriage is common, indeed the norm, and women in particular are expected to be married at a young age, the institution of marriage tends to take a bit of a beating. As noted, part of the expectation of marriage stems from the importance of children and childbearing in African cultures. In many relationships, however, the idea of a permanent, faithful marriage is often elusive, and infidelity, abandonment, and spousal abuse are frequent causes for divorce. Moreover, increasingly, larger numbers of young women are choosing to delay marriage and, instead, focus on obtaining an education and starting a career. Given the paucity of both educational opportunities as well as jobs, this should not be interpreted as a cultural sea change. Nonetheless, particularly in big cities like Lusaka and Ndola, other options may exist, and more and more women are taking control of their lives and futures. In the rural areas, however, there will be greater familial pressure on young women to get married.

Traditional Engagement Rites

Each of Zambia's major ethnic groups has distinct marriage rites and rituals, many of which continue to be practiced in spite of the other modern trappings of Zambian life. In some cases, these traditions have been preserved in modified form, often shortened or altered in other ways to fit within the confines of a modern existence (a full-time job, urban residence, convenience, and so on). Nonetheless, most retain their powerful symbolic value because they represent a vital connection to the culture of one's parents. This is especially important in urban areas like Lusaka with its great ethnolinguistic diversity and where many youth are increasingly enamored of Western norms and ideals.

Bridewealth

Bridewealth, sometimes called *lobola* or *nsalamo,* remains an essential feature of the marriage rites for the majority of Zambian cultures. It differs substantially in amount and function, however. In some cultures, such as the Bemba, the marriage payment, or *nsalamo,* was insignificant in terms of worth but, rather, was intended as a token to declare the would-be groom's intention to marry and to, in effect, start wedding negotiations. In earlier times, this was a nonmonetary payment, such as a bracelet or an axe, hoe, or some other tool. The custom is that it is presented by the aspiring groom's family to the father of the bride and the rest of her family. In traditional Bemba society, it was unlikely that the would-be groom would have met his future in-laws before this betrothal. In many circumstances it would be considered untoward for the parents of a prospective bride (or groom) to have gotten to know the intended before the initiation of formal negotiations. Indeed, even today, children seldom introduce boyfriends and girlfriends to their parents.

In some cultures, such as the Tonga, the bridewealth is of more significant value. Here, given the importance of cattle to Tonga culture, the payment is typically made in cows to the father of the bride. In any event, the purpose of the exchange should not be regarded cynically, as a get-rich-quick scheme on the part of fathers selling their daughters; rather, traditionally, it was viewed as a form of compensation for the lost labor that married daughters represented. Of course, girls leave their father's village to join their husband's; as a result, the father loses access to the labor that his daughter long provided. For the most part, however, *lobola* is symbolic. Yet it remains ripe for abuse, and in the contemporary period of growing international and domestic women's rights and advocacy campaigns it is sometimes controversial as well. Although not the intention, the higher the value of the payment, the greater the risk that the bride is viewed as a commodity, and de facto ownership of her passes from father to husband. Not surprisingly, this presents some genuine gender conflict, particularly in the contemporary period, as discussed later.

Another problem bridewealth gives rise to is the perception among men and women that they cannot marry without it. Others, however, will struggle to come up with the resources and may begin their marriages in financial straits. Again, if bridewealth is primarily symbolic rather than a transfer of wealth, this is not an issue, and many Westernized families will waive the payment altogether, or, increasingly, the Westernized children will refuse to participate.

Elopement is not unheard of, and, among the Tonga, elopement effectively ensures that the parents will consent to the marriage.[4] It is not a means of escaping the payment of *lobola,* however. In fact, Tonga (Southern Province) marriage traditions included elopement of bride and groom, with subsequent payment of bride wealth in the form of cattle. "Ideally, before marriage, the two families should meet and negotiate.... But after a couple has eloped, the families may meet to agree on the terms, or the parents of the girls may sue the man for damages and thus be compensated for the loss of lobola."[5]

Traditional Wedding Ceremonies

The Bemba have an elaborate set of rituals related to traditional marriage celebrations, most of which continue to be practiced today. Assuming the *nsalamo* is accepted by the prospective bride's family, the couple is thereafter considered betrothed. The next step is the *amatebeto*, a ceremony in which the bride-to-be's mother leads her female relatives, and often friends, in preparation of a feast consisting of a range of different dishes for the groom and his family and friends. Historically, this may have been done long, perhaps several months, before the wedding itself, although today it may be as little as a week prior to the actual wedding ceremony or may even take place after it. The bride's party will spend the entire day and night preparing a variety of traditional dishes. Then, leaving behind the bride *(banabwinga)*, who is forbidden to come, they will deliver the culinary bounty to the waiting groom and his entourage. The women dance and sing as they deliver the food. Each dish is presented to the groom, or *bashibwinga,* and part of the ceremony includes one of the celebrants washing the *bashibwinga*'s hands and feet. The groom is guided through the entire process by his *bashibukombe* ("father figure"), who is typically an older relative, such as an uncle, but not exactly immediate family. As trusted advisor, the *bashibukombe* interprets various aspects of the performance. The symbolism is important: In traditional times, these foods and the personal care (e.g., washing hands and feet) were what the new groom could expect from his bride in their married life.

Women prepare and deliver the food to the groom and his family as part of the *amatebeto.* Courtesy of the author.

The next ceremony is intended to be cloaked in secrecy and shielded from the uninitiated and unmarried. The *ubwinga* ceremony, often referred to as the "overnight" in English, served as the traditional wedding, after which the couple was considered married in the eyes of the community. As the English label implies, this ceremony occurs at night, and it includes both initiation rites *(cisungu)* for the bride and groom as a couple and separate trials and initiations for the bride alone. Moreover, although commonly referred to as the overnight in urban areas among middle-class Bemba practitioners, it is important to point out that a single night represents a significant abbreviation of the ritual; in rural areas, and certainly in the precolonial past, this ceremony would take weeks to complete. Even in contemporary urban environments "the initiation and wedding [can] take three days, with rituals performed in the bush on one day, rituals in the house over one evening and night with the coming out the following morning … [and] during the rite the women drink traditionally brewed beer *(katubi* and *katata)* … [and] at fixed periods food is served."[6] As in nearly all the marriage-related ceremonies, this one is replete with drumming, singing, and dancing.

The point of the *cisungu* is to teach couples the ways of marriage, and it is replete with metaphoric and symbolic references to sexual intercourse, pregnancy and child rearing, marital challenges, and the like. Because it is highly secretive, the specific traditions are not spoken of among the uninitiated. Thus, only the married relatives of the bride and groom, who have themselves been married through the *ubwinga,* are permitted to participate in the ceremony and even then, largely only as observers. The first part of the ceremony consists of the bride being kept in seclusion, for example in her bedroom. When the groom and his family arrive, the betrothed couple participates in a series of trials, led through the rites by the *banachimbusa,* a woman who is not usually a relative and, instead, is trained in this highly specialized role. After the couple has completed these trials, the groom and family depart, and the bride endures another long series of rituals, which last, at the very least, well until the morning hours of the following day.

As with all Zambia's ethnic groups, Bemba marriage ceremonies are a family affair. The *ukulula* ceremony takes place following the wedding, often the next day. The bride and groom sit on a woven cane mat *(ubutanda)* and receive blessings and counsel from the members of both families as well as from close friends. This very much resembles the receiving line common to many Western weddings, in which the bride and groom greet their guests for the first time as husband and wife and receive brief congratulations. A principal distinction, however, is that there is no time limit placed on the participants in the *ukulula,* which can, therefore, go on for hours with a large family.

After a set of rites that last several days, at the very least, often coupled with the planning and completion of a Western-style wedding and reception among many urbanized middle- and upper-class Zambian families, one would expect that the groom will have become fairly well acquainted with his new in-laws. Whereas this is literally true, figuratively speaking, despite paying *nsalamo* and enduring all the trials laid out for him, the new son-in-law is not considered fully admitted into his wife's family. The final ritual, *ukwingisha shifyala* (literally, "to let the son-in-law enter"), involves the ceremonial admission of the husband into the wife's family. This may not take place for several years after the actually wedding, and in some cases it may never occur. The intervening years between the *ubwinga* and the *ukwingisha shifyala* provide time for the couple to have children, and ensure stability in their marriage. According to a strict interpretation of the tradition, during this interim the husband is not permitted to dine with his wife's mother or enter the private quarters of the home for any reason. When the *ukwingisha shifyala* is completed, however, the son-in-law gains full acceptance into the family, and these prohibitions are lifted. Obviously, this is difficult to maintain in the context of a modern, more urban lifestyle, and many Bemba who otherwise adhere to long-standing cultural traditions tend to relax the strictures on this one. Nonetheless, this remains an important final ceremony of the marriage.

It is worth noting that few traditions have survived with no modifications from their origins; indeed, culture itself is not fixed. Moreover, although some of the traditions described are associated with a particular group, such as the Bemba or Tonga, it is important to recall that many of Zambia's ethnicities have similar provenance, as discussed in chapter 1. Hence, to the extent that cultural traditions associated with one group are borrowed by another today, it is tempting to regard this simply as a reconvergence of sorts, albeit after several centuries. One prominent example of this is the *amatebeto*. Once exclusively practiced in Northern Province by Bemba peoples, and to some extent in Eastern Province, the practice of *amatebeto* has been adopted—and adapted—by some Lozi couples, for instance, and, indeed, is now widely copied by members of other groups. Marriage between members of different ethnic groups has also resulted in the sharing of wedding traditions.

Western-Style Weddings

Of course, all Zambians, regardless of ethnic heritage, have been impacted by their encounters with Western norms and traditions, including those related to marriage. Nevertheless, couples are considered legally married in Zambia provided they go through the prescribed rites of passage for their group, some of which were described in the previous section. In many rural parts of Zambia especially, these marriages by traditional or customary law are all that exist. Many couples, however, will complete the traditional rites as well as a Christian wedding ceremony for religious reasons or a secular civil ceremony. Others, particularly those residing in larger cities and facing a barrage of Western influences, may opt to forego altogether Zambian marriage traditions in favor of Western ceremonies.

Civil marriages are done by means of registration with city or local officials. A fee is charged, and the couple must register in the presence of two witnesses; it is a simple, straightforward affair. Church-based weddings, by contrast, range from lavish affairs attended by hundreds of guests and conducted at the huge Anglican cathedral in Lusaka to modest ceremonies in small rural chapels. Church weddings typically are very much like their counterparts in the West and are guided by the liturgy of the particular faith or religious tradition. Stylistically, these weddings typically follow the Western pattern. Thus, one sees the familiar white wedding dress, tuxedoed groom and attendants, floral arrangements, wedding reception, and—at least among wealthier families— every move captured by a photographer and, perhaps, videographer. Many seem to follow from the same script: In Lusaka, for example, it is quite common to see a bridal party assembled amid the bougainvillea in the middle of a prominent traffic circle—a long-preferred site for wedding photos.

The Causes and Consequences of Divorce

In nineteenth-century North America and Europe, divorce was a rare occurrence. Even as recently as the 1950s, social and religious mores in the United States imposed fairly rigid restrictions on the dissolution of marriage; divorce was, at best, frowned upon. This was not the case in Zambia historically, where traditional marriage could be regarded as weak, at least in the sense that it could be dissolved with certain compensation by the man or the woman.[7] Especially in those Zambian cultures in which the payment of bridewealth was traditionally low, such as the Bemba and Kaonde, few alternatives were available to a man whose wife decided to leave him; there was little, if anything, that the man could demand to be repaid. Among the Tonga, however, there may be more resistance to dissolving traditional marriages through divorce. As one study of the Tonga observes, "Since marriage is seen as an alliance between the kin groups of husband and wife as well as a union between individuals, several factors act as preventives against a break in marriage. For instance, a wife's kinsmen have to return a substantial number of cattle to her husband before she can be freed from marital ties. This direct proprietary interest of the parents is expected to urge the daughter toward reconciliation of differences with the husband, while the husband is guided, principally, by his material interest."[8]

The diffusion of Christianity predictably altered the existing social mores about the right of divorce. Specifically, all the Christian churches frowned on, or in the case of Roman Catholicism, forbade divorce except in the most extreme circumstances. As in the West itself, however, many of these Western social and religious norms relating to marriage and divorce have been loosened in recent decades, particularly as women's empowerment has become an issue. Thus, today Zambians have, in a way, recaptured their traditional approach to marriage as a potentially impermanent relationship. Divorce is now fairly common, therefore, and seldom regarded as immoral or otherwise objectionable in and of itself; a divorce petition is seldom denied by the magistrate. Even Frederick Chiluba, the former president, is twice divorced, although, technically speaking, Chiluba and former First Lady Vera Chiluba obtained an annulment in 2001 after two decades of marriage. The Chilubas had been married under customary law. In any event, far less stigma is attached to divorce for men, though women may face more severe criticism within the society.

The causes of divorce are quite varied, and divorce cases may be brought by either the husband or the wife. A frequent basis for divorce relates to sexual matters, broadly, such as reproduction, performance, and fidelity. For example, men often will divorce their wives if the relationship has borne no children. Because the principal reason for marriage, particularly traditional or customary marriages but also many of those performed under statutory law, is procreation, the failure to produce children results in great sociocultural, community, and personal stresses on the couple. Ironically, regardless of which partner is infertile, the woman is usually the one deemed responsible for childlessness, although this is merely another indicator of the lower status of women in Zambian society.

Infidelity is another cause for terminating a marriage. As noted earlier in the chapter, there is a widespread (though hardly universal) expectation that men will cheat on their wives and girlfriends. Although this should not be misinterpreted as tolerance of such behavior, it is, nevertheless, uncommon to see women sue for divorce against philandering husbands. Fewer women than men tend to seek partnerships outside of their marriages (even if their husbands do), but that does not deter men from seeking divorce on these grounds. Interestingly, however, research on divorce among the Tonga, for example, revealed that if "loose morals were cited ... in most cases *wives* were found to be at fault."[9] This speaks more to legal and social biases against women than it does to a plethora of unfaithful wives.

Other reasons for divorce include spousal abuse, which is fairly commonly cited, despite the fact that there is a high social, if not legal, tolerance for such abuse, particularly in rural communities. Still others pertain to wives who are unwilling to have sex with their spouses or prepare food for their husbands; these actions are seen as a central part of the wifely role and are duties that women are often not at liberty to refuse. In terms of the former, especially, this has had a devastating impact on the spread of AIDS, as discussed later. In short, because women are seldom empowered to refuse their husbands sexually (or, equally, to insist on the use of condoms), the refusal to have sex or unprotected sex can result in divorce. At the same time, women's inability to negotiate sexual relations can have deadly consequences: The acquiescence to a roving husband's wishes can lead to HIV infection. These are hardly desirable choices, to be sure.

Simply because divorce is legally and culturally and religiously permissible is not to say, however, that couples have a cavalier attitude toward divorce or that there are not significant costs involved in going through it. Given the biases women face generally, it is not surprising that they may face both stigmatization from divorce as well as a potential loss of property and marital assets. Moreover, as women's work is primarily home-based, they face additional discrimination after marriages end. Customary law is typically biased against the woman in a divorce action. Women tend to lose property and, sometimes, social status as a result. The idea of maintenance or alimony is almost unknown in Zambia's customary law, although some research revealed that "certain lower courts in urban areas were ordering husbands to pay lump sums of 'compensation' on divorce. The purpose of these orders was partly to protect women who had been divorced without good cause and partly to compensate them for services they had rendered during marriage."[10] This compensation, however limited, offers at least some acknowledgment that women lose substantial assets and often need to find new residences when they divorce. Enforcement is weak, however.

Thus, even in the most urban settings, women may lose out to their ex-husbands, regardless of fault. As described for other areas of gender relations, there is an innate cultural bias that tends to forgive the male and his indiscretions, whereas the female may be punished, especially if she pursues the termination of the marriage. Thus, reports exist of women losing home and property to their ex-husbands and, occasionally, custody of her children. Moreover, the ex-husband may well orchestrate this de facto theft with the connivance of his relatives, including his female relatives. Although this lacks the force of law, uneducated women and poorer women in particular lack the recourse to the legal system, lawyers, police, and so forth. To be sure, this type of second-class treatment of women, although still too frequent, is increasingly challenged. A number of women's nongovernmental organizations, such as Planned Parenthood and the Family Life Movement, for example, and gender activists have worked hard to apprise women of their rights in the context of divorce as well as widowhood, abandonment, abuse, and so forth.

HIV/AIDS and Its Impact on Marriage, Family, and Gender Roles

The HIV/AIDS epidemic has had a devastating impact on marriage and families in Zambia. Estimated between 16 percent and 19 percent, the HIV-infection rate among the sexually active population has stabilized in recent years. Nonetheless, this still places the number of infected in the millions, a staggering number of infections in any country, let alone a poor country with an underdeveloped health care system and a population ill equipped to cope with the problem. Moreover, it has produced more than 600,000 orphans, by some estimates, and this has overwhelmed the capacity of families—let alone the state—to deal with them. Yet ordinary Zambians have confronted AIDS in an extraordinarily courageous way and continue to do so. Many of the orphans have been absorbed into families of uncles, aunts, and other relatives who already confront the disease and, typically, poverty within their own immediate families. This is the good news.

The bad news is that gender relations and the nature of the marriage relationship in Zambia have certainly contributed to the AIDS pandemic. As noted previously, many married men in Zambia have sex with women other than their wives. Girlfriends are hardly uncommon, even for prominent politicians, bureaucrats, and businessmen, let alone their less wealthy male counterparts in the compounds of the urban setting. As a result of multiple partners (and nearly all AIDS cases in Zambia, and in Africa as a whole, are spread through heterosexual intercourse), AIDS has spread like wildfire and devastated the dry, fragile tinder that constitutes many marriages. Of course, this is also true among sexually active single people as well. In either case, immediate families and extended families alike have suffered as a consequence. There is virtually no family in Zambia that can claim to be untouched by AIDS.

If a man contracts HIV from a woman who is not his wife, the chances are very high that he will transmit the virus to his wife before he himself becomes symptomatic. The wife has very little if any leverage in refusing her husband's sexual advances, as discussed previously. Thus, the sad irony is that even if she is aware of his sexual wanderlust, there is little she can do about it, save divorce. Yet divorce is not an option that most women pursue, and, if they do, it is usually too late, given that it may take approximately 6 to 10 years from initial infection to show symptoms. In short, what this amounts to is an elaborate game of sexual Russian roulette in which the outcome is just as grim.

A tradition known as cleansing, or *ukupianika* in iciBemba, still practiced in some rural communities, including among the Lamba people, threatens to continue the cycle of HIV/AIDS. In this tradition, after the death of her husband, a widow must be cleansed by a male relative of the husband, usually assigned by the chief. (The ritual also may be done on the death of a child.) Because a woman is considered to have married a family and clan and community as much as an individual, upon the death of her husband, she would not ordinarily return to her birth family but would remain instead in her late husband's village. The husband's nearest male relative, typically an elder brother or an uncle, would then inherit the widow, caring of her and her children as his own. In the precolonial, pre-Christian period, this nearly always resulted in the husband's kinsman taking his erstwhile sister-in-law as another wife. Although this continues in some areas today, more likely the widow will simply have to have sex with the surviving male relative.

Those who support this rite argue that it helps the woman avoid future promiscuity and that it appeases the spirit of the deceased. As seen in chapter 2, the importance attached to the spirit realm persists even in the contemporary period, and it is believed that if the deceased's wife is effectively abandoned, punishment will be visited upon the family. Thus, cleansing is in some ways a reflection of the strong bonds of community and of belonging. On the other hand, it is also indicative of the subordinate status of women, even widows, who are most vulnerable, who do not have the power to control their own bodies. In addition to this discriminatory aspect, obviously, in an age of HIV and AIDS, cleansing is a ritual that harbors potentially deadly consequences. First, the man selected to cleanse may himself be HIV-positive. It is not uncommon for the chief to select the same man for the job for years, and he may have contracted the disease himself. Second, the husband may have died of complications from AIDS, thereby putting the cleanser and his own wife and family at risk.

This practice has been condemned not only by foreign aid workers and AIDS activists but by Zambians themselves: everyone from NGO staffers to health professionals. The former minister of health, Professor Nkandu Luo, herself lambasted the continuation of cleansing at the 1999 International Conference on AIDS and sexually transmitted diseases in Africa, which was held in Lusaka. Health care workers and others have had an impact in some communities, notably the Tonga and Monge, whose chiefs have been prevailed upon in recent years to alter the practices. One way is to avoid sexual intercourse altogether by using purely symbolic methods of cleansing and inheritance. Indeed, given current realities in Zambia, this demonstrates greater respect for the dead as well as the living.

THE FAMILY

Notwithstanding the decidedly negative tone of the foregoing discussion—though, admittedly, it is impossible to put a positive spin on such issues as gender discrimination, divorce, and HIV/AIDS—it is possible, nonetheless, to conclude this chapter on the more positive subject of family life in Zambia. Indeed, even within the scope of the troubling issues previously discussed, the importance of family in Zambia resonates.

In Zambia, as in most of Africa, there is a broader understanding of family, such that the notion of a nuclear family consisting of father, mother, and children is an alien concept. Hence, grandparents, aunts, uncles, and cousins, both biologically near and distant, play critical roles in the lives of the children in this enlarged family unit. In fact, most Zambian languages do not even recognize the distinction between uncle and father, aunt and mother, or cousin and sibling.

In rural areas and more traditional settings, the idea of this expansive family is easier to maintain, and, indeed, it often extends to the entire village or settlement. The appropriation of the saying "it takes a village to raise a child" has made it sound trite, but communities take an active and collective role in the raising and disciplining of their children. The shared responsibility meant that, as discussed earlier, wives were never really widowed and children were never orphaned because they were absorbed into the larger family grouping. The unmitigated spread of HIV and AIDS has made caring for children who lose parents to the disease extremely difficult, and, to be sure, family structures are under threat from the disease; the existence of so many genuine orphans today is evidence of that. Yet one also sees extraordinary acts of kindness even in families that are financially destitute, which extend themselves and their homes to children even of fairly distant relatives.

Irrespective of HIV/AIDS, it is a challenge to maintain the traditional close-knit family structures in contemporary urban environments. Obviously, few families can afford to house their extended families beyond a handful of members. If relatives live in the vicinity, their regular interactions help preserve many of the traditional roles, norms, and language. Conversely, if the immediate family lives in Lusaka or Ndola and the extended family in Mongu or Chipata or Kasama, the collective family values that shape a child's identity, or an adult's for that matter, are potentially undermined. Wider communities have a strong incentive to promote these extended linkages, and families certainly endeavor to maintain them by encouraging urban relatives to travel home as often as possible.

Notes

1. Crehan, *The Fractured Community,* 133.
2. Saha, *History of the Tonga Chiefs and Their People,* 80.
3. Schlyter, *Recycled Inequalities,* 98.
4. Ibid., 93.
5. Ibid., 93.
6. Rasing, *The Bush Burnt,* 131.
7. Ibid., 43.
8. Saha, *History of the Tonga Chiefs,* 84–85.
9. Ibid., 83.
10. South African Law Commission, "The Harmonisation of the Common Law and the Indigenous Law."

7

Social Customs and Lifestyle

When Europeans began settling in what is now Zambia in the late nineteenth century, the combined influences of Christianity and colonialism led to the discouragement or outright banning of traditional ceremonies and cultural practices, which were erroneously regarded as heathen or threatening or both. At the same time, the economics of colonialism drove many people from villages to towns where, as part of new urban polyglots, they lost the social and cultural connection to many of their traditional practices. By the mid-1950s, therefore, many long-standing social customs and conventions had been altered or had disappeared altogether.

More than half a century later, Zambia is in the crosshairs of globalization, and Western influences in particular are plainly apparent, even dominant, whether in food, clothing, music, housing, gender relations, or religion, as other chapters in this book attest. Of course, many of these new cultural norms and individual modes of behavior have been around since before independence, with the expansion of new media—radio, cell phones, satellite television, Internet—and the freedom of movement—both of people and of commerce—that accompanied liberalization in the 1990s, the pace of change has certainly quickened in recent years. This dynamic environment is in many respects a double-edged sword. On one hand, it offers great opportunity, especially for individuals; on the other hand, however, it puts many Zambian traditions further at risk. Indeed, Zambian social customs both beneficial and arcane are under threat from an apparent juggernaut of Western cultural expansionism. These include not only relatively mundane things like what people eat but also the gerontocratic, or age-based, system that serves as a societal foundation, the important social markers that maturity and adulthood symbolize through initiation ceremonies, the institution of marriage, and so on. Indeed, these customs are what give Zambia its identity and its uniqueness.

Thus, the modern, largely urban contemporary lifestyle—importantly, not necessarily wealthy, by any means—has contributed to the erosion of social customs, at least since the colonial period. At the same time, the lifestyle of the vast majority of Zambians remains as it was decades ago and, in many cases, worse. In 1960, on the eve of independence, Zambia was among the richest of Africa's emergent postcolonial states. Affected by poverty, HIV/AIDS, political abuses, and the consequences of bad policy choices, Zambia's poor have good reason to be more concerned with the immediate demands of survival rather than with the preservation of traditional ceremonies and social customs.

Yet despite a largely hostile environment characterized by the twin pressures of globalization and domestic hardship—or perhaps because of it—many Zambians, both urban and rural, are finding solace as well as economic opportunity in their traditions. Thus, a number of Zambia's social customs and traditions are proving surprisingly resilient, if not expansionary. A clear trend exists toward the expression of renewed interest in the social customs of the various ethnic groups, a phenomenon that actually emerged on a smaller scale in the 1970s. Most people do not want to see these traditions die. Indeed, many have argued that the embrace of these traditions helps Zambians remain stable in turbulent times. Despite rampant poverty, the ravages of HIV/AIDS, and changing lifestyles, people have sought to reconnect with their past as a source of stability and identity.

In addition, a clear strand of entrepreneurialism runs through the renewed interest in age-old customs and ceremonies. Many of the traditional ceremonies and festivals have become not only national but international in scope, as the Internet, tourist guides, and improved access (through the proliferation of small private and charter airlines, for example) have exposed visitors to Zambia to activities that were sometimes guarded and/or restricted to members of the community in antiquity. Tour operators and ethnic communities themselves have recognized that culture *sells*, and as one group demonstrates success with this model, there is an incentive for others to follow. As a result, as of 2002, Zambia had some 20 and perhaps as many as 57 so-called traditional ceremonies of migration and conquest, offerings to ancestors, and so forth, and "the number increases yearly."[1]

Market incentives notwithstanding, this exposure to outsiders—not only foreign tourists but other Zambians, including invited politicians from different ethnic backgrounds—helps build cross-cultural appreciation and communication between communities. Indeed, given the common origins of many Zambians 500 or fewer years ago, many of the antecedents are shared, and thus more contemporary rituals reflect very similar traditions. This chapter begins with broader and increasingly public cultural celebrations before turning to the more specific rites and rituals surrounding female initiation, male circumcision, and burial that historically, at least, were restricted to participation by family and clan.

TRADITIONAL COMMUNITY CEREMONIES AND THEIR ORIGINS[2]

Kuomboka

With a history dating back more than three centuries, the Kuomboka is the best known of Zambia's traditional ceremonies. It attracts hundreds of visitors each year. Kuomboka, which means "to move to dry ground" in siLozi, the Lozi tongue, marks the annual migration of the Lozi king, the Litunga, and commemorates the Lozi settlement in western Zambia after they broke from the Lunda Empire in Congo around the early eighteenth century. They settled in the floodplains of the upper Zambezi River, where the first Litunga established his headquarters. For approximately three months each year, however, near the end of the rainy season, the floodplain is submerged.

A leading scholar of Zambia described the relationship of the Lozi people to their homeland and to their traditions:

> The great formative influence on the Lozi kingdom was the flood plain of the upper Zambezi. This is a sharply enclosed area of fertile land surrounded by the poor soils typical of western Zambia. During the dry season, when the river is low, the plain affords good grazing for cattle, and comparatively rich alluvial soil for cultivation; there are also patches of very favourable land along the plain margins. Thus parts of the plain have long supported unusually dense and stable settlements, in marked contrast to the scattered population of the surrounding woodland. Within the plain, people could cultivate the same plot year after year ... [but] as the flood-waters rise towards the end of the wet season, settlements become islands and must be abandoned.[3]

Thus, every year in late February or early March, the Lozi people bring their possessions and join their king as he travels from his winter residence at Lealui, near Mongu, to dry ground at Limulunga. A huge flotilla of thousands of boats and dugout canoes accompanies the Litunga amid great fanfare and drumming. Together with his attendants, paddlers, and drummers, the Litunga travels in his barge, Nalikwanda, downriver in a ceremonial journey that takes some six hours to complete. The Nalikwanda is directed by a group of some 30 or more paddlers in traditional dress, although the Litunga himself wears a somewhat more incongruous costume that at once indicates his historic power and illustrates the impact of Western culture.

An effective, highly centralized polity before colonialism, the Lozi kingdom was governed separately from the rest of Northern Rhodesia and given semiautonomous powers under the colonial name of Baroteseland. The British signed treaties with Litunga Lewanika, giving them suzerainty over the Lozi, and commemorated these treaties with a gift of a British admiral's uniform in 1902, on behalf of Queen Victoria. For more than a century, each successive Litunga has worn a replica of that uniform when he arrives at Limilunga. Upon completion of the journey, the people celebrate with traditional songs and dances. The ceremony lasts several days, allowing time for Lozi elders to arrive to pay homage to their king. Although the Litunga's powers, like those of all traditional rulers in Zambia, are circumscribed today, he continues to play a leading role in tribal governance and serves as the most prominent symbol of Lozi identity at the national level.

Mutomboko[4]

Meaning "crossing the river," the Umutomboko, or simply Mutomboko, is a two-day ceremony celebrated by the Lunda in Luapula Province. Almost all the Lunda peoples trace their origin to Lunda King Mwata Yamvo in what is today the Democratic Republic of the Congo (DRC). Under the leadership of Mwata Kazembe, the Lunda of Zambia migrated from Congo early in the eighteenth century, around 1740. Kazembe pushed eastward into what is today Zambia, defeated the Bwile and Shila and other peoples near Lake Mweru, and established the capital of a new kingdom there. According to tribal lore, each time the Lunda conquered a new group, they celebrated their conquest in the Mutomboko.

Led by the current Kazembe—an honorary title taken by successor Lunda kings, who follow dynastic rule passed from father to son—the Mutomboko marks the annual celebration every July of the migration from the DRC and commemorates the victories of Mwata Kazembe. Held in a village named Mwansabombwe, the celebration includes drumming, dances, speeches and performance, as well as tribute presented to the chief in the form of beer and food by the women. The ceremony concludes at an arena near the Kazembe's palace, where he performs the *umutomboko* or "royal dance of conquest." In contrast to the Bemba, for example, the Lunda remained a fairly cohesive group, and, with the advent of colonialism, they were not as deeply impacted by labor migration toward the copper mines. This may help explain the greater continuity of Lunda traditions throughout the colonial and postcolonial periods.

Ukusefya pa ng'wena

Interestingly, although they are Zambia's largest ethnic group, the Bemba people had substantially lost touch with many of their traditional community-wide rituals in a way that smaller groups such as Lozi, Ngoni, and Lunda had not. The reasons for this are threefold. First, the Bemba were the leading suppliers of labor to the copper mines. This migration depleted many Northern Province communities and severed innumerable ties with traditional practices. Second, around the time of independence, many Bemba people gained positions in government, the civil service, and small business in Lusaka and in the Copperbelt, further separating them physically and symbolically. Finally, community-wide cultural celebrations among the Bemba in particular were discouraged, not only by the colonial government but by President Kenneth Kaunda as well. Although he encouraged traditional ceremonies among most groups, Kaunda came to regard Bemba cultural nationalism as the basis for a rival political movement and a potential vehicle for his erstwhile liberation partner and later rival, Simon Mwansa Kapwepwe, whom he placed under arrest in 1972.

Even absent cultural celebration akin to the Lozi Kuomboka, however, the Bemba nonetheless maintained a distinct cultural identity, of which a major unifying features was not necessarily common language (iciBemba is also spoken by former subject peoples of the Bemba) but loyalty to the Chitimukulu, or paramount chief. Thus, it is not surprising that recent years have seen the Bembas recapture and revitalize their cultural programs, much as other groups have done. In fact, Mulenga Kapwepwe, the daughter of the late Simon Kapwepwe, has been among those active in promoting the recently revived Ukusefya pa ng'wena.

The Ukusefya pa ng'wena is the ceremony that celebrates the Bemba crossing, also from today's DRC, much like the similar celebrations of the migrations of neighboring groups. Ukusefya pa ng'wena means "celebrating a crocodile's land," the crocodile being an important totem among Bemba clans. According to legend, following the death of the founding leader, Chitimukulumpe, a dead crocodile was found on the land first settled in Zambia by the Bemba around the early seventeenth century. Although the historical record is inexact, scholars suggest, however, that the Bemba migration probably occurred in small groups over an extended period, hence the notion of a river crossing in one fell swoop celebrated in the Ukusefya pa ng'wena is based more on the founding myth of the Bemba people than on actual fact. Indeed, "the crossing of the Luapula [River] represents a transition from a fabulous primeval simplicity to the world of actual experience: the river marks a frontier between the unknown [past] and the known."[5]

Like many of the other contemporary expressions of ethnic identity and heritage by means of revived cultural celebrations, the Ukusefya pa ng'wena is intended to appeal to outsiders. (Indeed, the name of the ceremony was changed from Ukwanga pa Ngwena precisely because the word *ukwanga* was used by other groups.) Hence, Ukusefya pa ng'wena and similar programs serve a dual purpose: The commercial prospects and their appeal to tourists both domestic and foreign are an important corollary to the cultural dimension. Indeed, the Zambia National Tourist Board now lists all the major cultural ceremonies in its marketing of Zambian travel holidays.

Other Groups

As noted previously, nearly all Zambian ethnic groups can lay claim to a myth of origin and, at some point in their history, celebrated their beginnings. The Luvale of North Western Province, for example, hold a festival called Likumbi Lya Mize, or "the Day of Mize," which celebrates Mize, the ancient capital of the Luvale people. Held annually in July or August and lasting several days, the Likumbi Lya Mize features the renowned Makishi dancers, the group of young men who wear the elaborate masks known by the same name, which represent key figures in Luvale mythology. The Makishi dancers also perform at the Mukanda circumcision ceremony, described later. The related Chokwe people have a similar tradition.

Dancers in costume perform a Makishi initiation ceremony.
© Charles & Josette Lenars/CORBIS.

Among the Ngoni in Eastern Province, the annual gathering is called Nc'wala, or first fruits ceremony. Held in late February or early March, it draws thousands of Ngoni as well as observers to the Mutenguleni villages near the city of Chipata. In Southern Province, the Ila celebrate the Shimunenga annually in September or October. Participants in the three-day ceremony drive cattle across the Kafue River to symbolically reenact an important moment in Ila history when Shimunenga broke off from his brother, an important chief, to establish his own independent clan. In Ila lore, Shimunenga is regarded as a divine being who can bestow blessings upon crops and livestock and provides for the people. Like the other festivals, the Shimunenga is cause for much merriment—dancing, singing, and drinking—as well as an acknowledgment of a shared history. Finally, even the Lenje, a small ethnic group numbering only about 250,000 people, many of whom still make their home in Central Province, have an annual ritual. In the Kulamba Kubwalo, the Lenje pay homage to their chief and celebrate the harvest.

At bottom, wherever one travels in Zambia today, and practically whenever, a traditional cultural ceremony can be found. The proliferation and reinvention of these putatively ancient rites have simply led to a bandwagon effect; certainly no ethnic group wants to be regarded as insensitive to and disinterested in its heritage. Yet for smaller groups whose numbers and language are genuinely at risk, it may be a matter of promoting cultural awareness as a matter of survival.

INITIATION RITUALS

Rituals for Young Men

Various forms of initiation ceremonies for girls are practiced throughout Zambia, whereas, only a few groups practice any such rituals for boys. Like the cultural celebrations noted previously, these rituals have their roots in antiquity and are related to similar practices seen throughout central Africa. The Mukanda ceremony, a circumcision ritual for boys coming of age (historically at age 12 or 13) that marks their symbolic transition into adulthood, is celebrated in North Western Province among the Luvale and their related peoples, the Luchazi and Chokwe. Circumcision, however, is only part of the program, which may last between 6 and 12 months in total. The broader objectives of the Mukanda include teaching boys how to tend to their homes and households when they become men and signaling both the beginning of manhood for the initiate and the end of a mother's obligation to her son. Indeed, "the bond between mother and son, weakened after his circumcision wound has healed, is finally broken when the initiate leaves mukanda, and restrictions begin that prohibit mother and son from sitting or talking together in public."[6]

Like most of the initiation rituals for girls and boys alike, the proceedings are intensely private, access by nonparticipants is forbidden, and the sequestering of initiates is taken quite seriously. No women participate in the Mukanda. Moreover, as with some of the marriage traditions, the newly initiated are not permitted to provide details about their experiences with anyone outside the community and even with those who have not yet undergone the trials.

Rituals for Young Women

Virtually every Zambian ethnic group maintains coming-of-age rites for girls. Teenage rites take place around the girls' first menses, approximately age 12 or 13, although some, like the Kankanga initiation of the Ndembu, relating specifically to marriage and sexual techniques, are today more likely to be aimed at older girls and young women. Typically, girls are sequestered for the period of initiation, which can last as long as one to three months in the Lozi tradition (in modern times, this would be conducted during school holidays). Among the Lunda and Luvale, initiations once lasted as long as a year. Among the Bemba, Kaonde, Chewa, and Tumbuka, however, the *ic(h)isungu* may last as little as three days. In this latter tradition, a single girl is accompanied by one or more female elders *(banacimbusa),* usually chosen by her mother.

Even in contemporary urban environments, there are usually women known to the larger community who perform this role regularly; they are always mothers and wives and are considered wise and are respected. Girls are often sent back to the village, although among many urban families this is often done in the capital city as a matter of necessity. If possible, however, families may express a strong preference that girls return to their provincial homes and adhere rigidly to the traditions. Regardless of ethnicity, these initiations are centered on preparing girls to become women and, eventually, wives and mothers. The rituals, whose participants are entirely female, include both a celebratory dimension as well as tests of endurance and involve dancing, oftentimes bare-breasted, and the wearing of body paint, as per tradition.

Importantly, discussion about the so-called birds and the bees, although an acceptable, even desirable, parental role in many Western societies, is considered a completely inappropriate topic for discussion between parents and their children in Zambian cultures. Hence, the initiate's interactions with the *banacimbusa,* elders, or midwives almost invariably include sex education and may extend to instruction on explicit sexual techniques. Among some groups, however, such as the Bemba, the counsel just as often includes dire and often wildly exaggerated warnings about the perils of engaging in sex before marriage (it is worth recalling that these girls are only 12 or 13, well below marriageable age in contemporary times): "You will blow up," "your mother will die," and other similarly outlandish claims have been reported.

In short, sex and sexuality together form an essential dimension of the initiation process, and the training is significantly oriented toward pleasing the male partner. It is worth noting that one practice found elsewhere in parts of eastern, western, and Sahelian Africa, female circumcision (labeled female genital mutilation, or FGM, by critics of the practice), is not practiced in Zambian cultures. "Scarification and the stretching of the outer labia" are employed in some groups, however, such as the Luvale and Kaonde.[7] Elsewhere, such as in Eastern Province, young women are given instruction about how to tighten the vaginal opening through specific exercises and the use of traditional herbs.

Many traditions, such as those practiced by the Nsenga or the Ndembu, to name only two, require that the new initiates be presented to the community after the completion of the program in a sort of coming-out ceremony in which the young women are expected to perform dances, which are suggestive of her abilities as a sexual partner, and so on. In contemporary times, these can be quite public and not limited to the ethnic community; many celebrations have been covered in the national news media.

The early twenty-first century finds in these ceremonies a mix of contradictions. Many traditionalists, including prominent leaders in government, have called for the embrace of customs that hark back to the (often reimagined) pre-European past in order to reclaim lost heritages and avoid the homogenizing effects of globalization. On the other hand, a number of women's rights advocates, as well as conservative voices emanating from institutions such as the church, are critical of the traditional approach to girls' initiation, albeit for different reasons; the former suggest the practice perpetuates women's vulnerability and exploitation, whereas the latter argue it fosters promiscuity and immorality. The foundation for these criticisms is difficult to establish. Certainly, sexual permissiveness and promiscuity are genuine problems in the context of HIV and AIDS, particularly given their impact on young people, especially women. Yet the explicit sexual techniques learned by Nsenga initiates, and others, clearly need not lead them to try out their newfound skills prematurely, as some fear.

FUNERAL RITES

Contemporary funerals in Zambia tend to be similar to their Western counterparts, except that they typically last a number of days. As in other African countries, visitors and relatives travel to the home of the deceased and offer condolences to the surviving spouse and family. Instead of leaving, however, it is customary for mourners to remain at the home for some time, rather than simply pass through, which is generally regarded as disrespectful. Food is an important part of the funeral event, as mourners are considered guests in the home. In urban settings, however, the abundance of food and drink, coupled with the word-of-mouth nature of funeral announcements, can lead to occasional abuses: Many families can recount stories in which strangers simply dropped in on a funeral to take advantage of the abundance of food being prepared; only afterward does everyone learn that the individual had no connection to the deceased or his family. Although infamous, such instances of so-called gate-crashing at funerals are infrequent.

Close friends and relatives are expected to remain at the house overnight, with the men sleeping outside and the women sleeping on the floor (older women excepted) indoors, although some friends, and fewer relatives, who reside locally may return to their own homes to sleep if the quarters are too crowded. The burial does not take place within a specified period of time, as in some religious traditions; instead, the family will ordinarily wait for the arrival of relatives who are traveling some distance. The actual burial is a solemn event, but the procession to the burial site, by private cars or hired open-backed trucks, other vehicles, or on foot, is punctuated by singing. Several women will remain behind to prepare food for those returning from the interment site.

At the burial site, it is customary to lay flowers and remembrances on the grave. It has also become commonplace to cover graves with a slab of concrete because economic hardship has given rise to grave robbing, notwithstanding significant cultural taboos. Desperate, thieves are looking for everything from jewelry buried with the deceased to the suit in which he was interred. As in the U.S. context, the headstone, if one can be afforded, is added later, usually at the one-year anniversary of the death. Those who reside in urban areas, and certainly wealthier Zambians, employ the services of funeral homes, although in remote areas bodies will be washed according to traditional practice. Funerals for the majority of Zambian families could not be considered lavish, but they have been rather elaborate and time-consuming; they may, for example, require cross-country travel for surviving relatives or preparation of large amounts of food and, thus, great expense. As it has with so many aspects of life in contemporary Zambia, the AIDS epidemic has impacted death rituals. In large part because of the disease, the death rate has increased, and life expectancies have decreased drastically from 44 years in 1990 to only 33 years today. This means, quite simply, there are more funerals to attend than most people can afford.

NATIONAL AND RELIGIOUS HOLIDAYS

Zambia celebrates some 12 national holidays, among the more familiar of which include Christmas, Easter, New Year's Day, as well as the British-inspired Boxing Day. Zambians also celebrate Africa-specific holidays, such as Africa Freedom Day, which falls on May 25, and several that pertain specifically to Zambia, such as Farmers' Day on the first Monday in August and Zambian Independence Day on October 24. Although Christmas and Easter provide time for family celebrations and religious services relevant to the occasion, the Christmas period especially witnesses a great deal of social activity. Of course, the Christmas holiday is a time in most substantially Christian societies for good cheer and relaxation; it is perhaps particularly so in Zambia. First, the holiday season begins, for all intents and purposes, around early to mid-December and lasts up to four weeks. During this time, commerce slows considerably, as it is difficult to find businesspeople or workers on the job. Although constituency service is limited in Zambia's political system in any event, during the holiday season politicians, too, are likely to return to their home districts. Second, the first rains have nearly always begun by the holiday season. Thus, even in the rural areas, once seeds have been sown in anticipation of the rainy season, small-scale and subsistence farmers may have a brief respite before there the crop emerges.

Held every August in Lusaka, the National Agricultural Show is not simply a trade fair but a major social and cultural event. For several days, the exhibits, buildings, and grounds of the expansive Showgrounds in Lusaka, most of which are idle during the rest of the year, come alive with farmers, businesspeople, politicians, and ordinary citizens and their families. The majority of Zambians are dependent on farming, whether on the produce of the country's 400-odd commercial farm operations or on subsistence agriculture, which preoccupies the vast majority of Zambia's 600,000 small-scale farmers. With such an abundance of poor farmers, it would appear unlikely that an agricultural exposition would attract much of an audience. Surprisingly, however, year in and year out, the National Agricultural Show is a festival that not only attracts farmers from Zambia and the region but also draws far more attendees than only farmers. There are games and exhibits and carnival rides for children, agricultural demonstrations and awards, performances, food, and so on.

SPORTS AND SOCIETY

Football: Zambia's National Obsession

If Zambia can claim a national pastime, it is soccer. Known as football outside the United States, the game is played at every level, from the small village to international competitions. The latter draws an enormous fan base and unites the interests of Zambians throughout the country. Certainly, football has similar appeal across sub-Saharan and North Africa. Despite the poverty—or perhaps because of it—virtually every village in Zambia has at least a dirt soccer field, or pitch, bookended by a pair of makeshift goals. Indeed, football is a game ideally suited for a country of limited resources: It can be played on any hardscrabble field, and the game requires a modicum of equipment; if children do not have a ball, they will use tightly wadded rags, plastic bags, or whatever can be rolled into a spherical shape. Thus, the game is thoroughly nondiscriminatory in its availability, although it must be said that football is largely the preserve of boys and young men, rather than girls and women.

At the national level, the Football Association of Zambia (FAZ) governs competition between teams from various parts of the country, although most of the teams are based either in Lusaka or the Copperbelt. Both the teams and the local and national tournaments in which they compete are generally sponsored by local and international corporations doing business in Zambia—such as the Mosi (Zambian beer) Cup, the Coca-Cola Cup, and so forth—or national institutions—such as the Zambia Air Force–sponsored team, the Red Arrows.

The Zambian National Football Team, Chipolopolo, is perennial focal point for Zambians of all ages and socioeconomic backgrounds. Chipolopolo has enjoyed international recognition; many players participate in more

Boys practicing soccer techniques with a ball made of woven plastic bags. © Gideon Mendel/CORBIS.

lucrative national leagues in other countries, in South Africa and Europe, for example, and some of Zambian players, such as Kalusha Bwalya, have earned spots on teams in the premier leagues in Europe and are regarded as bona fide heroes back home. Internationally, the Zambian team has placed near the middle of world rankings according to the international football federation (FIFA): In 2005 they ranked 66th worldwide, for example, whereas they ranked 63rd in December 2001. In recent years, Chipolopolo has not advanced very far in the biennial African Cup of Nations (Africa Cup); however, the team did place second in 1992 and third in 1996, and in 1994 it reached the quarterfinals. Nor has it qualified for the World Cup tournament. Yet the team's performance has done little to dampen the enthusiasm of the Zambian citizenry for both the players and the sport.

In April 1993, the entire team was lost when the plane carrying them to a World Cup qualifying match crashed off the coast of Gabon. There were no survivors; all 18 players aboard were killed—18 of the 19 members on the national team—together with their coach and 10 other passengers and crew. The military transport plane was en route to Dakar, Senegal, when it crashed shortly after a refueling stopover in Libreville, Gabon. According to reports of the accident, the plane had earlier experienced mechanical problems after its departure from Lusaka and, in fact, had not been in use for nearly a year before it was pressed into service on behalf of the national team. After one engine caught fire and failed, the pilot, reportedly fatigued, inadvertently shut down the wrong engine, causing the plane to plunge into the Atlantic Ocean less than a half-mile offshore.

Although the official explanation was equipment failure compounded by pilot error, the accident raised a furor for grief-stricken Zambians as well as a host of rumors and conspiracy theories. One view that gained prominence was that the then particularly highly regarded Zambian team was actually shot down to prevent it from advancing to the World Cup and from winning the Africa Cup. Others wondered why team captain Kalushya Bwalya was not on the plane (playing professionally in the Netherlands, he had been scheduled to meet his teammates in Senegal). The country entered a period of national mourning; however, many questions emerged about the nature of the accident, and, given the scope of the tragedy, few were satisfied with the official response. Furthermore, families of the players complained that they were never fully compensated for the losses by the government and that the investigation by the Guinean government covered up culpability.[8]

A new team was rapidly put together to fulfill Zambia's participation in the 1994 World Cup qualifiers, but it narrowly lost to Morocco in Casablanca. The Zambian side reached the finals of the Africa Cup several months later, however, losing narrowly to Nigeria. Nonetheless, the improbable performance by the substitute team made them the darlings of the tournament and earned the new players national hero status in Zambia.

Other Sports

At the provincial and national level, competitive sports in Zambia is surprisingly well organized, with federations governing each sport. For all, funding is a perennial concern, and business and other sponsorship, not only for the teams themselves but also for national tournaments and participation in international tournaments, is essential to allow competitive sports to function. Yet outside of football, funding is more difficult, and national fan interest is not nearly as great.

The supply of players can also be problematic because the opportunity to participate in many sports from a young age is circumscribed by time, poverty, and facilities. Moreover, as with football, Zambia exports much of its athletic talent; many players wind up playing professionally or semiprofessionally in other countries. Nonetheless, Zambians field domestic teams and have leagues in a variety of sports, including track and field (athletics), boxing, basketball, and rugby, with athletics and basketball attracting women's teams as well as men's. All of these sports compete internationally, particularly in the southern and eastern African regions. Zambia also sends teams to the Olympic Games, which have provided another source of both entertainment and national pride. For example, track star Samuel Matete won the silver medal in the 1996 Olympic Games in Atlanta, Georgia, in the men's 400-meter hurdles, the highest placement ever for a Zambian at the Olympics. Not since Keith Mwila won bronze in the 1984 summer Olympic Games had Zambia even laid claim to a medal. Importantly, there is growing interest and skill in a variety of sports in Zambia in recent years, and since the 2000 Olympics, in addition to boxing and men's and women's track and field (and football, if the team qualifies), Zambia has also fielded teams in swimming.

Although fielding a competitive team in any professional or semiprofessional sport is expensive, and funding a league sometimes prohibitively so, other sports face even more severe limitations in Zambia. Sports like football, athletics, to some extent boxing, and so forth are egalitarian and democratic. Whereas training requires particular time and dedication, and therefore may involve significant cost, nothing explicitly bars individuals from participating in such sports. Yet athletes face obvious limitations of facilities, training, equipment, and so on for many other sports activities. Not surprisingly, therefore, the participants in more expensive and more elaborate sports are largely of a higher socio-economic class than the majority of Zambians for whom few alternatives exist besides football. These would include, most prominently, golf—a sport with obvious colonial roots, but played increasingly by businesspeople, politicians, and members of the expatriate community—as well as tennis, squash, cricket, and competitive swimming, given the paucity of sizable pools.

SOCIAL ACTIVITY AND NIGHTLIFE

Zambia has countless bars, restaurants, and clubs. Found in every province, in virtually every municipality, these range from fancier private clubs and the upscale service of the international hotels to brew pubs to unlicensed and unregulated shebeens (beer halls) or hole-in-the-wall establishments with few or any amenities, except perhaps a few stools or plastic chairs, though even these usually have music and dancing. Similarly, the restaurant scene ranges from expensive establishments visited only by businesspeople and politicians to so-called takeaways that consist of little more than an ordering window. Both ends of the scale can be crowded and immensely popular with its target clientele.

The music-oriented clubs in Zambia, which offer recorded and sometimes live music, can easily be described as vibrant. In the most popular venues, patrons stand shoulder to shoulder to reach the bar or, just as often, the dance floor, where they find DJs who play a mix of U.S. hip-hop, European techno, Zambian and other African rhythms at ear-splitting volumes. Live musicians, principally Zambian artists but also those from Congo and elsewhere, will play in clubs or concert venues like the popular Mike's Car Wash in Lusaka. The scene is typically mixed. Although mostly young, upper-middle-class black Zambians certainly predominate, members of the Asian community, with its relatively higher disposable income, and expatriates are among the regular clientele. In addition, it is not unusual to find middle-aged and older men at clubs ostensibly geared toward a younger crowd; although many of them are married, they may be there, unsurprisingly, on the prowl for young women. Conversely, cultural stigmas virtually ensure that women of any age will seldom go to clubs alone. Instead, a woman will go with friends, male or female. As noted in an earlier chapter, married women, particularly those who are mothers, tend to be little seen at bars and discos. This is another example of gender inequity in Zambia.

An interesting aspect of the club scene, despite its vibrancy, is the fickle nature of Zambian interests. The 1990s, for example, saw a wave of new clubs—with names like Moon City, Black Velvet, Cosmopolitan, Zorba the Greek—come and go with astonishing regularity, especially in Lusaka. Almost as quickly as one new club opened its doors, yesterday's magnet closed its doors. The pattern appears to have continued in the years since. Often, however, these clubs and discos are owned by the same people; with the ability to respond quickly to fickle tastes, they cycle new establishments in and out, clearly cognizant of the fragile nature of club popularity in the country.

It is important to distinguish between urban and rural establishments as well as those that cater to a relatively wealthy minority versus those whose principal clientele is poor, or certainly poorer than most of those who frequent the clubs already described. Whereas urban nightlife appeared to thrive and had a certain vibrancy even in the depths of the 1990s economic downturn, this same level of activity simply does not take place in rural areas. Constraints imposed by money, irregularity of electrical power, and the nature of rural work, such as farm labor or subsistence and its requirement for early mornings, can make for a vastly different lifestyle. Thus, although young urbanites may enjoy all the trappings of twenty-first-century partying, their rural counterparts may live an existence not altogether different from generations ago. If drink is available, it is as likely to be home brew as it is "shake-shake" or Mosi beer. Entertainment and nightlife in the far-flung areas of Zambia may simply entail listening to a radio and sharing stories.

NOTES

1. As reported by the Zambian Ministry of Community Development. Gordon, "The Cultural Politics of a Traditional Ceremony," 64.

2. Note that, as with ethnic group names, there are various accepted spellings of these ceremonies, depending on the transcription.

3. Roberts, *A History of Zambia*, 97.

4. This section draws heavily on the analysis of Gordon, "The Cultural Politics of a Traditional Ceremony."

5. Roberts, *A History of the Bemba*, 48.

6. Jordan, *Chokwe!*, 82.

7. Ibid., 78.

8. See "ASN Aircraft Accident Description."

8

Music and Dance

The performing arts in Zambia, specifically music and dance, are like other aspects of the country's culture and customs in that they represent a mix of traditions and influences and that they have been in considerable flux at least since independence in 1964. Thus, Zambian music is quite varied, but few discernible forms endure today that have deep historical roots. Nonetheless, it is important to acknowledge that there are clearly some connections between traditional and modern, or contemporary, music and dance in Zambia, however vague the antecedents. These caveats notwithstanding, this chapter divides the subject of music and dance between those forms and variations associated with particular cultural traditions, many of which are deeply historical, and more contemporary forms unattached to a specific rite or cultural tradition and performed (or participated in) mainly for entertainment purposes. Reflecting their origination in different eras, of course, the former are dominated by non-Western, decidedly low-tech instrumentation and accompaniment, whereas the latter styles of music and dance employ more sophisticated technologies in performing as well as recording.

Of course, music and dance in Zambia are at least as old as the diverse cultures that inhabit it. Zambia has a rich tradition of drumming and, as noted in chapter 2, of singing and dancing performance related to religious services, both Christian and non-Christian. Similarly, dances emerged out of cultural celebrations and initiations, although, even in the pre-European era, they also were performed principally as a source of entertainment. As noted in chapter 7, many of these traditional performances were discouraged during the colonial period as backward, heathen, or even evil because they were seen as threatening to colonial authority or simply because they were misunderstood. Yet, beginning with independence, many have been revived, and the pace of their recovery, and in some cases, reinvention, accelerated in the 1990s. Partly, this serves to reconnect Zambians with their ancient heritage, or what they perceive as their heritage, and partly because traditional songs and dances can have genuine entertainment value: Visitors to Zambia increasingly represent an opportunity for Zambian communities to attract tourist dollars by promoting so-called authentic African tribal dances.

The contemporary music and dance scene is witnessing a similar expansion as new styles are adopted or created by Zambian performers and the mainly young people who support them. To some degree, contemporary music and dance in Zambia are obviously influenced by traditional practice. For example, the dances many girls learn as part of their initiations and so on inform or certainly influence their sense of rhythm. To a lesser extent, the use of traditional instruments, such as the drums, the thumb or finger piano, and the xylophone-type instrument called the *silimba* also have a precolonial origin. Yet it is almost impossible to calculate how much traditional infuses the modern and equally difficult to discern the uniquely Zambian cultural and historic origins of contemporary music and dance in Zambia.

This is contrary to a number of other well-known musical genres. Despite their diverse origins (including roots in Africa), familiar musical genres such as soukous, samba, and jazz are nonetheless grounded to a substantial degree

Women drummers at a traditional ceremony. Courtesy of the author.

These women welcome visitors to a local clinic and school with a performance. Courtesy of Megan Simon Thomas (2005).

in the particular cultures that refined them and made them famous, in these cases, Congolese, Brazilian, and African American, respectively. In contrast, contemporary music in Zambia generally lacks a distinctive sound or a distinctive dance that one can readily identify as Zambian, although Zambian song lyrics are typically in a local tongue.

TRADITIONAL FORMS OF MUSIC AND DANCE

Nearly all of the ceremonies described in earlier chapters, whether related to initiation, marriage, or other activities, involve music. The use of drums is intrinsic to most ceremonies, and, in many instances, other instruments are used, and singing, either by participants or spectators or both, is also quite common. Moreover, dancing is embedded in most celebrations and traditional rites of passage, as seen, for example, in the traditions of the masked Makishi dancers who inhabit characters of Luvale mythology and whose elaborate dances are instrumental in the Mukanda circumcision ritual. In short, singing and dancing take place in all of these age-old customs; although some of these, or at least certain aspects, are intensely private, each activity is participatory. Others, like the *mganda* dances of the Tumbuka, which are open to the community, are purely for the enjoyment of the participants and the entertainment of the audience.

The Nyau Society

The Nyau secret society is a tradition of the Chewa people, who reside in Eastern Province and more extensively in neighboring Malawi, although in more recent times, young men from the Kunda and Nsenga ethnic groups have also participated. Nyau has religious origins, and its chief function is to revere ancestral spirits. These spirits are depicted in the masks that the all-male Nyau members wear in the course of their performances, which historically were conducted at events such as funerals and girls' initiation rituals. Males are initiated into the Nyau society as teenage boys. Among the skills and training initiates are expected to master are construction of huts, mask-making, and survival techniques, but they also learn to perform dances, to drum, and to mime as part of their performance duties. The elaborate costumes worn in the Nyau ceremonial dancing include individual masks that completely obscure the identity of the participants, but it is not uncommon for villagers to know who is a Nyau member.

Historically, the dance was even performed in secret, with physical harm, or threats thereof, coming to those who intruded on the performance. Nonetheless, local villagers would watch surreptitiously because the dances were so extraordinary and enjoyed great mystique. The dances can be symbolic, suggestive, or menacing, depending on the character each dancer portrays, such as an old man, a woman, a warrior, and so on. Lyrics to the songs that accompany the Nyau dances round out the portrayals and carry important meaning.

As with innumerable customs and traditions among Zambian peoples, the Nyau dances were discouraged during colonialism. The dances, the fearsome masks, the intimidation of outsiders and threats of violence against intrusion on the ceremonies, and their association with ancestral spirits led the colonial government to regard Nyau as the embodiment of black magic and anti-Christian behavior. Beginning in the 1950s, however, the Nyau dances were revived and received further encouragement with the transition to independence in the 1960s. The reemergent Nyau ritual, however, was largely devoid of the threats of physical violence against any uninitiated outsiders who dared attempt to observe the proceedings, a change partly encouraged by the Kaunda government. Indeed, the Nyau today is widely witnessed by spectators and performed at cultural expositions around the country. It is a cultural performance, which, though certainly not unmoored from its basis in Chewa traditions, has undergone the injection of a considerable degree of commercialism.

Mganda Dances

The Mganda dances stand out as a thoroughly modern invention, that is, a practice whose origins lie only in the post–World War II period rather than in some unspecified primordial past. Thus, this relatively recent tradition among the Tumbuka people of Eastern Province represents music and dance for the sake of entertainment.[1] The origins of Mganda lie in the return of Tumbuka men to the area following the war, wherein they had been conscripted by the British Army. Trained to march and drill military style, they adapted and Africanized these forms for Tumbuka audiences, preserving aspects such as alignment of the dancers. In fact, *ganda* means "to march like soldiers" in the language spoken by the Tumbuka.

The Mganda is performed by men, typically young men, between May and November, following the harvest but before the rainy season and the planting of new crops. This is a time of year that the residents of the community have relatively idle time to enjoy entertainment; Mganda groups representing different villages will frequently compete against one another. Unlike the secretive Nyau of the neighboring Chewa, the Mganda was always intended as a public performance, and the audience participates in the spectacle, encircling the dancers, who perform to the sounds of drumming and a kazoolike instrument called the *baja*, fashioned from a gourd. The dance is accompanied by song, whose lyrics range from political to humor to social commentary.

The Kankanga Dance

In Northwestern Province, the Ndembo have long practiced an initiation ritual that prepares girls for marriage. The initiate, historically a girl in her early teens, is referred to as Kankanga. In the pre-Christian period, it was expected that all Ndembo girls would participate in this ritual. This ritual, too, however, is subject to the same dynamic forces that affect all aspects of culture and customs in Zambia today; hence, some will choose to opt out of the ceremony, apparently without reproach.

As traditionally practiced, the dance itself represented the culmination of a three-month-long process of isolation for the initiate in which, under the direction of a midwife, she was trained about sex, marriage, and motherhood. The dance, therefore, is a central part of the coming-out ceremony in which the girl is introduced as a woman and a wife. A Western anthropologist who witnessed the Kankanga dances in the mid-1950s described it in the following manner:

She dances: her hand is gracefully fanning a black swirl of animal hair over her shoulder—the headman's fly switch. She is one rapid vibration from heel to skirt to shoulders, so that her breasts flash up and down, while her head falls languorously from side to side. Even her back is jingling, for now she is wearing a back pad stitched all over with bells which resound every time she shakes her back. She is a percussion system in full swing, she and the drums along with the frenzied singing.[2]

This was referred to in English as the "breast dance," and, indeed, the fixation on the breasts differs from dances that form part of the initiation process for girls from Eastern Province communities. There, the dances tend to be more explicitly focused on the pelvic area and, arguably, more sexually suggestive.

As with the Nyau dances, these rituals suffered from colonialism and were discouraged by Christian missionaries; consequently, the number of women who could serve as midwives to guide initiates diminished, and many Ndembos stopped the practice altogether. The Ndembo are a small group in Zambia, located in the least accessible, most underserved province in the country. This almost certainly played a role in both the relatively late period that the Kankanga began to decline—the 1950s—and the relatively late period in which it experienced a cultural revitalization: the 1980s.[3] Yet this resurgence has come with important modifications to the earlier model, including adaptations from neighboring cultures. For example, Lozi praise dances are now embedded in the Kankanga as well as songs taken from Luvale, Kaonde, and Lunda sources. Moreover, the initiate now routinely performs the dance fully clothed, and the ritual can represent as little as a simple coming-out party. It is still common, however, for the village to observe the ceremony and for song and dance to occur among the women assisting the Kankanga. Drums and a harplike instrument continue to figure importantly in the proceedings.

CONTEMPORARY MUSIC AND DANCE

Contemporary music and dance in Zambia can only be described as eclectic. Performing artists incorporate various recognizable influences from the West and elsewhere in Africa; however, there are surprisingly few discernible elements of the music and dance traditions discussed in the previous section. Among the Zambian features expressed in music are, of course, Zambian-language lyrics and the call-and-response singing style (which, admittedly, is hardly confined to Zambia). An interesting innovation, although also found in other African countries, is the injection of music, particularly drumming and singing, and dancing into the conservative Christian liturgy set down in Zambia by Western missionaries. In addition, the popularity of gospel music, hymns, and Christian-themed pop music sung in vernacular tongues has grown, particularly alongside expanded interest in charismatic churches in Zambia.

Regardless of the genre, however, it is difficult to identify a particularly unique, distinctly Zambian sound. As performance art, musical styles borrow heavily from Congolese rumba, U.S. jazz, Jamaican reggae, and, in more recent years, ragga, rap and hip-hop, gospel, as well as South African pop music. The closest one comes to indigenous contemporary music in Zambia is a genre known as *kalindula,* a form that emerged in the late 1970s and early 1980s and made popular by groups such as the Uweka Stars and Serenje Kalindula, each of which attracted a huge domestic following. *Kalindula* is essentially a brand of pop music, characterized by guitar riffs and Zambian vernacular. In fact, it is mainly defined not by the music itself but by the way in which one dances to it: Its fast-paced dance moves emanate from the waist, in a sort of side-to-side, circular pattern.

Kalindula was perhaps a consequence of a political decree issued by President Kenneth Kaunda in 1975 requiring that 90 percent of radio airtime be devoted to original Zambian music, with foreign artists relegated to the remaining 10 percent. Certainly, this served as a state-sponsored promotion of Zambian artists and the Zambian music scene generally. Indeed, notwithstanding the authoritarian nature of the decree, in practice it was a boon to Zambian artists and performers, who immediately saw their work promoted and given airtime by the state-owned broadcaster, ZNBC, which at that time controlled the only radio stations in the country.

The demand for other music, however, from Congolese rumba or soukous to country and western, which is also popular, remained strong, and with the eventual relaxation of the 90 percent requirement in the 1980s, these and other non-Zambian genres once again made playlists, though they were always popular in people's homes where a record or cassette player was available.

Music is heard on ZNBC and, now, private radio stations like Radio Phoenix as well as through music videos broadcast on both local and satellite television. Nationally prominent acts perform often at venues in Lusaka and the Copperbelt, and lesser-known performers frequently can be found in the bars and small clubs found in many Zambian towns. Not surprisingly, however, because Zambia is a mostly poor country, a comparative few people own cassette players (or the means to consistently power them with batteries or electricity), and fewer still own compact disc players or more cutting-edge technologies. Given the limitations of this domestic market, the music-recording industry is quite small, with only a handful of studios, promoters, and distributors. Nonetheless, it is always possible to find cassette tapes of Zambian recording artists in most urban markets. The use of compact discs is expanding far more slowly than in the West (where the technology is increasingly outmoded), but CDs are finding a market among consumers.

Despite the comparatively small population of potential CD buyers, which acts as a financial constraint for new music promoters and recording studios to enter the business, there appears to be a strong domestic interest in hearing Zambian artists. Zambian music enjoys a great—and growing—popularity within the country. Indeed, many musicians actually credit President Kaunda's decree with jump-starting the Zambian music business and creating a domestic audience. State-owned ZNBC not only played artists it also became the major studio recorder. The late Akim Simukonda, Rikki Ililonga, and the Mulemena Boys were popular acts in the 1980s, for example. Singer Jane Osborne has enjoyed a following for many years. In the late 1990s and early 2000s, artists such as JK, MC Wabwino, Black Muntu, and Danny, among others, have been able to build on the legacy of Zambia's pioneer musicians, issuing multiple albums and performing regularly around the country.

The local music industry reached its nadir in the early 1990s, commensurate with the country's economic collapse. By that time, state-owned ZNBC no longer had the resources to support indigenous artists, and the few private-sector recording studios that emerged in the 1960s and 1970s had all but disappeared. Today, the entertainment company Mondo Music has emerged as the major player on the Zambian music scene, promoting new artists and providing opportunities to promising performers. Mondo Music's growing catalog includes not only the most recent releases based on the Zambian variant of Jamaican ragga but also local rhythm and blues (R&B) and what the company describes as "some good old *kalindula*."

The strong interest in Western and other Africa music remains, yet the competitive position—both supply and demand—of Zambian music has improved markedly since the 1990s. Then, Zambian artists found themselves at a disadvantage, competing typically against U.S. or South African artists, for airtime on local radio. In urban dance clubs that catered to a middle- and upper-class clientele, even Zambian musicians were difficult to find because DJs showed a preference for U.S. R&B and hip-hop and the latest South African tunes. Even in smaller, less well-heeled venues, listening preferences tended toward Congolese rumba. Barely a decade later, the local flavor is much more apparent.

International Reputation

Thus far, although a few Zambian bands and solo artists perform regionally, most remain little known outside the country's borders and perhaps even in some parts of Zambia itself. Yet this situation is changing, albeit slowly, with the proliferation of the Internet (Mondo Music, for example, has a comprehensive Web site), satellite television and music videos, and the popularity of programs like *Afropop Worldwide,* which airs weekly on public radio in the United States and exclusively features African artists. Moreover, increased international travel, both to Zambia (which has attracted steadily increasing annual tourist traffic since troubled neighbor Zimbabwe is no longer an attractive destination) as well as by Zambians has accelerated the proliferation of Zambian music around the globe.

The progress has been relatively slow, however, for talented Zambian artists who are anxious to expand their listening audience. Singers such as Jane Osborne and JK are among those who have played European and U.S. venues as well as other African countries. Others, like Anna Mwale and Rikki Ililonga, left Zambia to establish themselves elsewhere. Zambia has yet, however, to export a genuine international music star with virtually global name recognition as have some other African countries: Cameroon's Manu Dibongo, Salif Keita of Mali, Miriam Makeba and Hugh Masekela of South Africa, or Nigeria's Fela Kuti come to mind.

These performers gained international acclaim for various reasons: Some established a base in Europe or the United States; some, like Miriam Makeba, sang in English about the tribulations of apartheid-era South Africa and thus attracted a following; others, like Fela, gained cult status, in part because of his politically charged lyrics (a style eschewed historically by Zambian musicians) and partly through dissemination by the substantial Nigerian diaspora. Zambian performers have yet to establish these kinds of connections, either with foreign audiences or with the business side of the music industry, although with time they may yet penetrate international markets.

NOTES

1. See Tembo, "Chinaka."
2. Turner, "Zambia's Kankanga Dances," 61.
3. The dates are suggested by Turner, who observed the Kankanga at 30-year intervals and describes the changes but without offering an explanation for the variance with the decline and resurgence of other ethnic traditions in Zambia.

Glossary

Note that some words have multiple spellings, depending on the dialect.

amatebeto (**also** *matebeto*). A ceremony in which a bride-to-be's mother leads her female friends and relatives in the preparation of a feast for the groom and his family and friends.

baja. Kazoo-like instrument used during the Tumbuka's Mganda dance.

banabwinga. Bemba term for "bride."

banacimbusa. Bemba term for a female elder who accompanies a girl during her initiation rites and is specially trained to guide betrothed couples through a series of trials as part of the wedding ceremony.

bashibukombe. Bemba term for an advisor or father figure, typically an older relative, who guides a groom through the marriage process.

bashibwinga. Bemba term for "groom."

buhobe. Lozi term for *nshima*.

chikanda. Bemba term for a traditional dish known as "African baloney" for its shape, consistency, and color; made from orchid tubers, chilies, groundnuts, salt, and baking soda.

chinaka. Nyanja term for *chikanda*.

chitenge. Colorful printed cloth worn by Zambian women.

Chitimukulu. The paramount chief of the Bemba people.

cisungu. Bemba term for initiation rites accompanying the wedding ceremony.

citemene/chitemene.   Slash-and-burn agriculture.

ic(h)isungu.   A term for female initiation used among the Bemba, Kaonde, Chewa, and Tumbuka.

ifikubala.   A tasty snack of large caterpillars dried, fried in oil, and eaten as a side dish.

Ifyabukaya.   "Things that you know"; also the name of a radio program that offers stories in the Bemba language.

kalindula.   A style of pop music featuring Zambian lyrics that emerged in the 1980s.

Kankanga.   An initiation ritual of the Ndembu for girls coming of age, relating specifically to marriage and sexual techniques.

katata **similar to (***katubi***)**   Traditionally brewed beer.

Kulamba Kubwalo.   Ceremony of the Lenje to pay homage to their chief and celebrate the harvest.

Kuomboka.   Lozi term meaning "to move to dry ground"; an annual ceremony that marks the migration of the Lozi king and commemorates the Lozi settlement in western Zambia after they broke off from the Lunda Empire in Congo in the early eighteenth century.

kwacha.   Zambian currency.

Likumbi Lya Mize.   Luvale celebration of "the Day of Mize," the ancient capital of the Luvale people.

Litunga.   The Lozi king.

lobola.   Widely used term for bridewealth in southern Africa.

lushimi.   A Bemba word meaning "fable" or "legend."

Makishi.   Group of young male dancers who wear elaborate masks known by the same name, which represent key figures in Luvale mythology.

manzi.   Nyanja term for water.

mganda.   Male dance style that emerged in the post–World War II period among the Tumbuka people of Eastern Province.

miombe.   Woodland, which consists of tall grasses, trees, and shrubs and covers two-thirds of Zambia.

mopani.   Elephant grass.

Msene.   Senegalese occasionally used in reference to black Muslims.

Mukanda.   A circumcision ritual for boys coming of age that marks their symbolic transition into adulthood; practiced in North Western Province among the Luvale and their related peoples, the Luchazi and Chokwe.

musisi.　Traditional costume worn by Lozi women.

Mutomboko (also Umutomboko, Mutumboko).　Lunda term meaning "crossing the river"; a ceremony celebrated annually to commemorate the eighteenth-century migration of the Lunda people from what is today the Democratic Republic of the Congo.

Nalikwanda.　A barge used by the Lozi king during the Kuomboka ceremonies.

Nc'wala.　Annual gathering or first fruits ceremony celebrated by the Ngoni in Eastern Province.

ndiwo.　A relish eaten with *nshima,* composed of meat and vegetables or at least gravy of some kind.

ngulu.　Bemba nature spirits that represented the rocks or waterfalls and received offerings from hereditary priests.

nsalamo.　Bemba term for bridewealth.

nshima.　Zambian staple food; a stiff dough or mash made from ground corn.

nyau yolemba.　Chewa mask type characterized by large zoomorphic basketwork structures that represent wild animals as well as cars, cattle, sorcerers, and Europeans.

Nyau.　A male secret society of the Chewa people whose chief function was to revere ancestral spirits.

Phochedza M'Madzulo.　"To hang around in the evening"; the name of a popular Nyanja language radio broadcast of the 1970s and 1980s.

rondavel.　Round hut with a thatched roof.

salaula.　Inexpensive secondhand clothing imported from abroad.

Shimunenga.　Ceremony of the Ila that commemorates the establishment of an independent clan.

silimba.　Zambian xylophone-type instrument.

ubutanda.　A woven cane mat on which a bride and groom sit to receive blessings and counsel as part of the *ukulula.*

ubwali.　Bemba term for *nshima.*

ubwinga.　Traditional Bemba wedding ceremony, often referred to as the "overnight" in English, which includes initiation rites and trials for the bride and groom.

ukulula.　A Bemba ceremony that takes place following the wedding in which the bride and groom receive blessings and counsel from family members and friends.

ukupianika. Bemba term referring to the outmoded custom in which a widow must be cleansed by (i.e., have sex with) a male relative of her deceased husband.

Ukusefya pa ng'wena. A Bemba term meaning "celebrating a crocodile's land"; a commemoration of the Bemba migration from what is today the Democratic Republic of the Congo. Previously called Ukwanga pa Ng'wena.

ukwingisha shifyala. "To let the son-in-law enter"; marks the ceremonial admission of a new husband into the wife's family.

Selected Bibliography

"ASN Aircraft Accident Description de Havilland Canada DHC-5D Buffalo—Atlantic Ocean off Gabon." *Aviation Safety Network.* November 29, 2003. April 15, 2006. http://aviation-safety.net/database/record.php?id=19930427-2&lang=en.

Bamberger, Michael, Bishwapura Sanyal, and Nelson Valverde. "Evaluation of Sites and Services Projects: The Experience from Lusaka, Zambia." *World Bank Working Papers* 548 (1982).

Bond, G. C. *The Politics of Change in a Zambian Community.* Chicago: University of Chicago Press, 1976.

Bread of Life Church, International. "About Us." July 22, 2005. http://www.blci.org.zm/aboutus.html.

Burnell, Peter. "The Party System and Party Politics in Zambia: Continuities Past, Present and Future." *African Affairs,* 100 (2001): 239–63.

"Call for Zambian Law on Genetically Modified Organisms." Panafrican News Agency (PANA) Daily Newswire, July 25, 2002.

Cancel, Robert. *Allegorical Speculation in an Oral Society: The Tabwa Narrative Tradition.* Berkeley and Los Angeles: University of California Press, 1989.

Chabal, Patrick, and Jean Pascal Daloz. *Africa Works: Disorder as Political Instrument.* Bloomington: Indiana University Press, 1999.

Chanock, M. *Law, Custom and the Social Order: The Colonial Experience in Malawi and Zambia.* Cambridge: Cambridge University Press, 1985.

Chauncey, George. "The Locus of Reproduction: Women's Labour in the Zambian Copperbelt, 1927–1953." *Journal of Southern African Studies,* 7.2 (1980/1981): 135–64.

Ciekaway, Diane, and Peter Geschiere. "Confronting Witchcraft: Conflicting Scenarios in Postcolonial Africa." *African Studies Review,* 41.3 (December 1998): 1–14.

Collins, John. "Lusaka: The Historical Development of a Planned Capital, 1931–1970." *Lusaka and Its Environs: A Geographical Study of a Planned Capital City in Tropical Africa.* Ed. Geoffrey J. Williams. Lusaka: Zambia Geographical Association, 1986. 95–137.

Colson, E. *Marriage and the Family among the Plateau Tonga of Northern Rhodesia.* Manchester, U.K.: Manchester University Press for Rhodes-Livingstone Institute, 1958.

Colson, E., and T. Scudder. *For Prayer and Profit: The Ritual, Economic and Social Importance of Beer in Gwembe District, Zambia, 1950–1982.* Stanford, CA: Stanford University Press, 1988.

Crehan, Kate. *The Fractured Community: Landscapes of Power and Gender in Rural Zambia.* Berkeley and Los Angeles: University of California Press, 1997.

Cunnison, Ian George. *The Luapula Peoples of Northern Rhodesia: Custom and History in Tribal Politics.* Manchester, U.K.: Manchester University Press, 1959.

"Divorce for Zambia's First Couple." *BBC News Online.* Septemper 25, 2001. June 15, 2005. http://news.bbc.co.uk/2/hi/africa/1562488.stm.

"Eaten as Food, African Orchids Threatened by Illegal Trade." *Science Daily.* August 1, 2001. July 23, 2006. http://www.sciencedaily.com/releases/2001/08/0108 01081646.htm.

Ellison, Gabriel, and The Zambia National Visual Arts Council. *Art in Zambia.* Lusaka, Zambia: Bookworld, 2004.

Elmslie, W. A. *Among the Wild Ngoni; Being Some Chapters in the History of the Livingstonia Mission in British Central Africa.* New York: Revell, 1899.

Epstein, A. L. "The Network and Urban Social Organisation." *Social Networks in Urban Situations: Analyses of Personal Relationships in Central African Towns.* Ed. J. C. Mitchell. Manchester, U.K.: Manchester University Press, 1969. 77–117.

Epstein, A. L. *Urbanization and Kinship: The Domestic Domain on the Copperbelt of Zambia, 1950–1956.* New York: Academic Press, 1981.

Ferguson, James. *Expectations of Modernity: Myths and Meanings of Urban Life on the Zambian Copperbelt.* Berkeley and Los Angeles: University of California Press, 1999.

Fomunyoh, Chris. "Democratization in Fits and Starts." *Journal of Democracy* 12.3 (2001): 37–50.

Fredson, Steven M. *Dancing Prophets: Musical Experience in Tumbuka Healing.* Chicago: University of Chicago Press, 1996.

Geisler, Gisela. "'A Second Liberation': Lobbying for Women's Political Representation in Zambia, Botswana and Namibia." *Journal of Southern African Studies* 32.1 (2006): 69–84.

Gertzel, Cherry. "Introduction." *The Dynamics of the One-Party State in Zambia.* Eds. C. Gertzel, C. Baylies, and M. Szeftel. Manchester, UK: Manchetser Univeristy Press, 1984.

Gordon, David M. "The Cultural Politics of a Traditional Ceremony: Mutomboko and the Performance of History on the Luapula (Zambia)." *Society for Comparative Study of Society and History* 46.1 (2004): 63–83.

Hall, Richard. *Zambia.* London: Pall Mall Press, 1966.

Hansen, Karen Tranberg. *Keeping House in Lusaka.* New York: Columbia University Press, 1997.

Hansen, Karen Tranberg. *Salula: The World of Secondhand Clothing and Zambia.* Chicago: University of Chicago Press, 2000.

Hantuba, Muna. "Government Policy on Agriculture." *TheZambian.com.* 2004. February 20, 2006. http://www.thezambian.com/agriculture/government. aspx.

Heisler, H. *Urbanisation and the Government of Migration: The Inter-Relation of Urban and Rural Life in Zambia.* New York: St. Martin's Press, 1974.

Hinfelaar, Hugo. *Bemba-Speaking Women of Zambia in a Century of Religious Change (1892–1992).* Leiden, NY: Brill, 1994.

Ho, Mae-Wan. "Zambia Will Feed Herself from Now On." *Science in Society* 17 (2003): 6–9.

"Hungry Zambians Eat Dog as Famine Deepens." Panafrican News Agency (PANA) Daily Newswire, October 4, 2002.

Ilukena, Namasiku. "Zambia Church Banned for 'Satanism'." *Mail and Guardian,* September 9, 1998.

"Industries in Zambia." *TheZambian.com.* 2004. January 20, 2006. http://www. thezambian.com/zambia/industries.aspx.

Johnson, Walton R. *Worship and Freedom: A Black American Church in Zambia.* New York: African Publishing, 1977.

Jordan, Manuel, ed. *Chokwe! Art and Initiation among the Chokwe and Related People.* Munich: Prestel, 1998.

Jules-Rosette, B. "Changing Aspects of Women's Initiation in Southern Africa: An Exploring Study." *Canadian Journal of African Studies* 13.3 (1979): 389–405.

"Kabwe Muslims Vow to Vote for Levy." *The Times of Zambia* (Ndola), March 7, 2006.

Kaswende, Kingsley. "There Is Excessive Beer Drinking in Zambia—Masebo." *The Post* (Lusaka), February 28, 2006.

Lamb, Christina. *The Africa House: The True Story of an English Gentleman and His African Dream.* New York: HarperCollins, 2004.

Lehmann, Dorothea. *Folktales from Zambia (Texts in Six African Languages and in English).* Berlin: Dietrich Reimer, 1983.

"Let's Develop Zambia, Levy Tells Muslim Society." *The Times of Zambia,* February 4, 2004.

Luig, Ulrich. *Conversion as a Social Process: A History of Missionary Christianity among the Valley Tonga, Zambia.* Hamburg, Germany: Lit Verlag, 1997.

Macmillan, Hugh, and Frank Shapiro. *Zion in Africa: The Jews of Zambia.* London: I. B. Tauris, 1999.

Marwick, Max. *Sorcery in Its Social Setting: A Study of the Northern Rhodesia Cewa.* Manchester, U.K.: Manchester University Press, 1965.

Mathews, Robin. "Chitemene, Fundikila and Hybrid Farming." *TheZambian.com.* 2004. February 20, 2006. http://www.thezambian.com/agriculture/farming. aspx.

McCaffrey, Oona. "The Nyau Dance." *The Drama Review* 25.4 (1981): 39–42.

Mingochi, D. S., and S.W.S. Luchen. "Traditional Vegetables in Zambia: Genetic Resources, Cultivation and Uses." *Department of Agriculture, National Irrigation Research Station, Mazabuka, Zambia.* April 21, 2006. http://www. ipgri.cgiar.org/Publications/HTMLPublications/500/ch20.htm.

Murphy, Ian, and Richard Vaughn. *Zambia.* London: Corporate Brochure, 1994.

"Music of Zambia." *Art History Club: Art History Web Reference and Guide.* 2005. April 19, 2006. www.arthistoryclub.com/art_history/Music_of_Zambia.

Mytton, G. "Language and the Media in Zambia." *Language in Zambia.* Ed. Sirarpi Ohannessian and Mubanga E. Kashoki. London: International African Institute, 1978.

Parpart, Jane L. "'Where Is Your Mother?': Gender, Urban Marriage, and Colonial Discourse on the Zambian Copperbelt, 1924–1945." *International Journal of African Historical Studies* 27.2 (1994): 241–71.

"The People of Zambia." *Guide to Zambia, Zambia National Tourist Board.* 2004. March 26, 2006. http://www.zambiatourism.com/travel/hisgeopeop/people. htm.

Phiri, Brighton, and Joe Kaunda. "AAGM: Don't Allow GM Maize in Absence of Policy—ZNFU." *The Post* (Zambia), October 16, 2002.

Rakner, Lise. *Political and Economic Liberalisation in Zambia: 1991–2001.* Uppsala, Sweden: Nordiska Afrikainstitutet, 2003.

"Rap, Ragga and Reggae in Nairobi, Dar es Salaam and Lusaka." *Musikmeet: The Stockholm Music Museum.* April 28, 2006. http://www.musikmuseet.se/ mmm/africa/lusaka.html.

Rasing, Thera. *The Bush Burnt, the Stones Remain: Female Initiation Rites in Urban Zambia.* Piscataway, NJ: Transaction, 2002.

Reynolds, B. *Magic, Divination and Witchcraft among the Barotse of Northern Rhodesia.* London: Chatto and Windus, 1963.

Richards, A. I. *Land, Labour and Diet in Northern Rhodesia.* London: Oxford University Press, 1939.

Roberts, Andrew. *A History of the Bemba: Political Growth and Change in North-Eastern Zambia before 1900.* Madison: University of Wisconsin Press, 1973.

Roberts, Andrew. *A History of Zambia.* New York: Africana, 1976.

Rooke, Andrew. "Kuomboka: Ancient Wisdom of the Malozi." *Sunrise,* 29 (5) February 1980: 174–78.

Saha, Santosh C. *History of the Tonga Chiefs and Their People in the Monze District of Zambia.* New York: Peter Lang, 1994.

Schlyter, Ann. *Recycled Inequalities: Youth and Gender in George Compound, Zambia.* Uppsala, Sweden: Nordiska Afrikainstitutet, 1999.

Seshamani, Venkatesh. "A Hindu View of the Declaration of Zambia as a Christian Nation." *Jesuit Centre for Theological Reflection* 46 (2000). April 21, 2006. http://www.sedos.org/english/seshamani.htm.

Sinyangwe, Binwell. *A Cowrie of Hope.* Oxford: Heinemann Educational, 2000.

South African Law Commission. "The Harmonisation of the Common Law and the Indigenous Law." *Discussion Paper 74: Customary Marriages.* August 1997. August 10, 2005. http://wwwserver.law.wits.ac.za/salc/discussn/dp74. html#N_452_#N_452_.

Spitulnik, Debra, and Mubanga E. Kashoki. "Bemba: A Brief Linguistic Profile." April 22, 2000. June 30, 2004. http://www.anthropology.emory.edu/faculty/ANTDS/Bemba/profile.html.

Spitulnik, Debra. "Radio Culture in Zambia: Audiences, Public Words, and the Nation State." Unpublished Ph.D. dissertation, University of Chicago, 1994.

Spitulnik, Debra. *Semantic Superstructuring and Infrastructuring: Nominal Class Struggle in ChiBemba.* Bloomington: Indiana University Linguistics Club, 1987.

Tait, John. *From Self-Help Housing to Sustainable Settlement: Capitalist Development and Urban Planning in Lusaka, Zambia.* Aldershot, U.K.: Avebury, 1997.

Tembo, Mwizenge S. "Chinaka: Traditional food of the Tumbuka." April 28, 1997. March 25, 2006. http://www.bridgewater.edu/~mtembo/chinaka.html.

Tembo, Mwizenge S. "The Mganda Traditional Dance among the Tumbuka of Zambia." July 27, 1995. March 25, 2006. http://www.bridgewater.edu/~mtembo/mugandadance.html.

Tembo, Mwizenge S. "Mice as a Delicacy: The Significance of Mice in the Diet of the Tumbuka People of Eastern Zambia." March 25, 2006. http://www.bridgewater.edu/~mtembo/mbeba.html.

Tembo, Mwizenge S. "*Nshima:* Zambian Food Staple." March 25, 2006. http://www.bridgewater.edu/~mtembo/nshimachapter1.htm.

Teuten, Timothy. *A Collector's Guide to Masks.* Secaucus, NJ: Wellfleet, 1990.

"Traditional Ceremonies." *Guide to Zambia, Zambia National Tourist Board.* 2004. April 24, 2006. http://www.zambiatourism.com/travel/hisgeopeop/tradcere.htm.

Turner, Edith. "Zambia's Kankanga Dances: The Changing Life of a Ritual." *Performing Arts Journal* 10.3 (1987): 57–71.

Turner, V. W. *The Forest of Symbols: Aspects of Ndembu Ritual.* Ithaca, NY: Cornell University Press, 1967.

Van Binsbergen, Wim M. J. *Religious Change in Zambia: Exploratory Studies.* Monographs from the African Studies Centre, Leiden. Boston and London: Kegan Paul International, 1981.

White, C.M.N. "Factors in the Social Organisation of the Luvale." *African Studies,* 14 (1959): 97–112.

"Zambia." *Committee to Protect Journalists.* 1997. Septemper 15, 2005. http://www.cpj.org/attacks97/africa/zambia.html.

"Zambia." *Grove Art Online.* 2006. Online Dictionary of Art. Oxford University Press. July 25, 2005. http://www.groveart.com.

"Zambia: Arts and Literature." *Cultural Profiles Project, Citizenship and Immigration Canada.* 2000. March 26, 2006. http://cp.settlement.org/english/zambia/arts.html.

"Zambian Institutions Back Government on Rejected Maize from U.S." Panafrican News Agency (PANA) Daily Newswire, August 1, 2002.

"Zambian Muslims Urged to Vie for Political Positions." *The Post* (Zambia), January 30, 2006.

Zulu, Brenda. "Drought Shuts Zambia's Door to GMOs." *Mail and Guardian Online,* April 22, 2005. April 15, 2006. http://www.mg.co.za/articlePage.aspx?articleid=235875&area=/insight/insight_africa/.

Index

About the Author

SCOTT D. TAYLOR is Assistant Professor, School of Foreign Service and African Studies, at Georgetown University.